OWASP TOP 10 VULNERABILITIES

BEGINNER'S GUIDE TO WEB APPLICATION SECURITY RISKS

4 BOOKS IN 1

BOOK 1
WEB APPLICATION SECURITY 101: A BEGINNER'S GUIDE TO OWASP TOP 10 VULNERABILITIES

BOOK 2
MASTERING OWASP TOP 10: A COMPREHENSIVE GUIDE TO WEB APPLICATION SECURITY

BOOK 3
ADVANCED WEB APPLICATION SECURITY: BEYOND THE OWASP TOP 10

BOOK 4
THE ULTIMATE OWASP TOP 10 HANDBOOK: EXPERT INSIGHTS AND MITIGATION STRATEGIES

ROB BOTWRIGHT

Published by Rob Botwright
Library of Congress Cataloging-in-Publication Data
ISBN 978-1-83938-629-9
Cover design by Rizzo

Disclaimer

The contents of this book are based on extensive research and the best available historical sources. However, the author and publisher make no claims, promises, or guarantees about the accuracy, completeness, or adequacy of the information contained herein. The information in this book is provided on an "as is" basis, and the author and publisher disclaim any and all liability for any errors, omissions, or inaccuracies in the information or for any actions taken in reliance on such information. The opinions and views expressed in this book are those of the author and do not necessarily reflect the official policy or position of any organization or individual mentioned in this book. Any reference to specific people, places, or events is intended only to provide historical context and is not intended to defame or malign any group, individual, or entity. The information in this book is intended for educational and entertainment purposes only. It is not intended to be a substitute for professional advice or judgment. Readers are encouraged to conduct their own research and to seek professional advice where appropriate. Every effort has been made to obtain necessary permissions and acknowledgments for all images and other copyrighted material used in this book. Any errors or omissions in this regard are unintentional, and the author and publisher will correct them in future editions.

BOOK 1 - WEB APPLICATION SECURITY 101: A BEGINNER'S GUIDE TO OWASP TOP 10 VULNERABILITIES

BOOK 2 - MASTERING OWASP TOP 10: A COMPREHENSIVE GUIDE TO WEB APPLICATION SECURITY

BOOK 3 - ADVANCED WEB APPLICATION SECURITY: BEYOND THE OWASP TOP 10

BOOK 4 - THE ULTIMATE OWASP TOP 10 HANDBOOK: EXPERT INSIGHTS AND MITIGATION STRATEGIES

Introduction

In an increasingly digital world, web applications have become the lifeblood of modern businesses and services, serving as gateways to countless online interactions. However, this digital dependence has also exposed us to a myriad of security risks and vulnerabilities that can have far-reaching consequences. As cyber threats continue to evolve, the need for robust web application security has never been more critical.

In this comprehensive book bundle, "OWASP Top 10 Vulnerabilities," we embark on a journey that spans the entire spectrum of web application security. From novice learners to seasoned experts, our collection of four distinct books caters to individuals at every stage of their security journey.

"Book 1 - Web Application Security 101: A Beginner's Guide to OWASP Top 10 Vulnerabilities" serves as the perfect entry point for those new to the world of web application security. We'll take you by the hand and introduce you to the essential concepts, demystifying the notorious OWASP Top 10 vulnerabilities along the way. This book provides a solid foundation upon which you can build your security knowledge.

In "Book 2 - Mastering OWASP Top 10: A Comprehensive Guide to Web Application Security," we dive deeper into the realm of web application security. Here, we provide a comprehensive guide that empowers you to understand

and master the intricacies of the OWASP Top 10 vulnerabilities. Whether you're an intermediate learner looking to strengthen your skills or a seasoned professional seeking a comprehensive resource, this book has you covered.

"Book 3 - Advanced Web Application Security: Beyond the OWASP Top 10" takes us on a journey beyond the familiar OWASP Top 10 list. We explore advanced security concepts, emerging threats, and in-depth mitigation strategies. This book is designed for those who crave a deeper understanding of web application security and wish to stay ahead of the curve in a constantly evolving landscape.

Our final installment, "Book 4 - The Ultimate OWASP Top 10 Handbook: Expert Insights and Mitigation Strategies," brings together the wisdom and experiences of industry experts. These thought leaders provide invaluable insights and real-world strategies that bridge the gap between theory and practice. This book serves as a beacon for those who aspire to become true security champions.

Throughout this book bundle, we emphasize the profound importance of web application security. In today's interconnected world, the protection of sensitive data, user privacy, and organizational assets hinges on our ability to defend against evolving threats. Our books aim to equip you with the knowledge and tools to safeguard web applications effectively, regardless of your expertise level.

As we embark on this journey through the "OWASP Top 10 Vulnerabilities" book bundle, remember that the quest for web application security is not only a necessity but a shared responsibility. We invite you to immerse yourself in these pages, absorb the insights, and embark on a transformative journey toward becoming a guardian of the digital realm.

Join us as we explore the depths of web application security, from its fundamental principles to its most advanced strategies. Together, we can fortify our digital world against the ever-persistent forces of cyber threats and vulnerabilities.

BOOK 1
WEB APPLICATION SECURITY 101
A BEGINNER'S GUIDE TO OWASP TOP 10
VULNERABILITIES

ROB BOTWRIGHT

Chapter 1: Introduction to Web Application Security

Web application security is a paramount concern in today's digital age, as the internet has become an integral part of our lives, touching almost every aspect, from communication and entertainment to shopping and banking. With the increasing reliance on web applications, there is a growing need to protect sensitive information and ensure the privacy and safety of users. In recent years, we have witnessed numerous high-profile data breaches and cyberattacks that have exposed the vulnerabilities in web applications, highlighting the critical importance of robust security measures. These incidents have demonstrated that no organization, regardless of its size or industry, is immune to the threats that lurk in the digital realm. Web application security encompasses a wide range of practices, technologies, and strategies aimed at safeguarding web applications from various threats, including hackers, malware, and other malicious entities. It involves not only protecting the data that users input into web applications but also securing the underlying infrastructure and preventing unauthorized access to sensitive systems. The consequences of failing to address web application security can be severe, resulting in financial losses, reputational damage, legal ramifications, and, most importantly, harm to individuals whose data may be compromised. In addition to the potential legal and financial consequences, a security breach can erode trust and confidence in an organization, causing customers to lose faith in its ability to protect their information. In today's interconnected world, where data is often the lifeblood of businesses and individuals alike, such breaches can have far-reaching and long-lasting effects. Furthermore, web application security is not solely about mitigating external threats; it also involves ensuring that applications function correctly and are resilient to unexpected issues. Poorly secured web applications can be susceptible to downtime, crashes, and other disruptions that can disrupt business operations and lead to customer frustration. To address these multifaceted challenges, organizations must adopt a proactive and holistic approach to web application security. This approach begins with a comprehensive understanding of the potential threats and vulnerabilities that web applications face. By identifying and assessing these risks, organizations can develop a tailored security strategy that addresses their specific needs and priorities. An essential aspect of web application security is staying up-to-date with the latest threats and attack techniques, as the digital landscape is constantly evolving. Hackers are continually devising new ways to exploit vulnerabilities, and security professionals must be equally vigilant in their efforts to counter these threats. The Open Web Application Security Project (OWASP) Top 10 is a widely recognized resource that provides a list of the most critical web application security risks. It serves as a valuable reference for organizations looking to prioritize their security efforts and focuses on vulnerabilities that are commonly exploited by attackers. Among the OWASP Top 10 vulnerabilities are injection attacks, broken authentication and session management, cross-site scripting (XSS), and security misconfigurations, to name a few. Understanding these vulnerabilities and how to mitigate them is essential for anyone involved in web application security. Additionally, web application security encompasses a range of best practices and security measures, including secure coding practices, regular security testing and assessments, and the implementation of security controls such as firewalls and intrusion detection systems. Secure coding practices involve writing code with security in mind, from the initial design phase through to development and maintenance. This includes using input validation to prevent injection attacks, implementing strong authentication and access control mechanisms, and validating and encoding output to prevent XSS vulnerabilities. Regular security testing and assessments involve evaluating web applications for vulnerabilities and weaknesses using various techniques, such as penetration testing, code reviews, and vulnerability scanning. These tests help identify and remediate security issues before they can be exploited by malicious actors. Furthermore, the use of security controls, such as firewalls and intrusion detection systems, can provide an additional layer of defense by monitoring and filtering incoming traffic to detect and block potential threats. While these security measures are essential components of a web application security strategy, it is crucial to recognize that security is not a one-time effort but an ongoing process. As new vulnerabilities emerge, organizations must adapt and update their security measures accordingly to stay ahead of potential threats. Moreover, it is not only the responsibility of security professionals to ensure web application security but a collective effort that involves developers, system administrators, and other stakeholders. Developers play a critical role in writing secure code and adhering to best practices, while system administrators are responsible for configuring and maintaining the infrastructure that supports web applications. Effective communication and collaboration among these roles are essential for building and maintaining secure web applications. In summary, web application security is a fundamental aspect of the digital landscape, and its significance cannot be overstated. The protection of sensitive information, the preservation of user trust, and the avoidance of financial and reputational damage all depend on the implementation of robust security measures. Organizations must recognize the evolving nature of web application threats and take a proactive approach to address these challenges effectively. By understanding the risks, adopting best practices, and staying informed about the latest threats, organizations can build and maintain secure web applications that withstand the ever-present dangers of the   digital   world Key concepts in web application security provide the foundation for understanding and implementing effective security measures in the digital realm. These concepts encompass a wide range of principles, strategies, and best practices that are crucial for safeguarding web applications against a myriad of threats and vulnerabilities. One of the fundamental concepts in web application security is the principle of defense in depth, which involves implementing multiple layers of security controls to protect against various attack vectors. By employing multiple layers of defense, organizations can mitigate the risk of a single point of failure compromising the security of their web applications.

Authentication and authorization are essential concepts that revolve around the verification of user identities and the determination of their access privileges. Proper authentication ensures that only authorized users gain access to sensitive resources within a web application, while robust authorization mechanisms control what actions these users are allowed to perform. Another critical concept is input validation, which involves thoroughly validating and sanitizing user inputs to prevent injection attacks, such as SQL injection and cross-site scripting (XSS). Input validation is a fundamental practice in writing secure code and is instrumental in preventing malicious data from compromising the integrity of web applications.

Cross-site scripting (XSS) and cross-site request forgery (CSRF) are two prominent security vulnerabilities that merit special attention. XSS vulnerabilities occur when untrusted data is included in a web page's content, potentially allowing attackers to execute malicious scripts in the context of unsuspecting users. In contrast, CSRF vulnerabilities involve tricking users into executing unintended actions on web applications without their consent. Both XSS and CSRF vulnerabilities require meticulous mitigation strategies to prevent exploitation and safeguard user data and privacy.

Security misconfigurations are yet another significant concept in web application security, often resulting from incorrect or incomplete configuration settings. Attackers actively seek misconfigured components, such as databases, web servers, or cloud storage, as entry points to exploit vulnerabilities and gain unauthorized access. Therefore, proper configuration management and regular security assessments are vital for identifying and rectifying these security misconfigurations.

Secure communication and data protection are paramount in web application security, and encryption plays a crucial role in achieving these objectives. Transport Layer Security (TLS) is a commonly used encryption protocol that ensures data exchanged between the client and the server remains confidential and tamper-resistant. Furthermore, encrypting sensitive data at rest, such as user passwords and payment information, is essential to protect against data breaches and unauthorized access to stored information.

The concept of threat modeling involves systematically identifying and assessing potential threats and vulnerabilities in web applications. By creating threat models, organizations can prioritize security efforts, allocate resources effectively, and proactively address security risks before they can be exploited by attackers. Threat modeling is a dynamic process that evolves as web applications and their associated threats change over time.

A fundamental principle in web application security is the least privilege principle, which dictates that users and systems should be granted only the minimum level of access or permissions necessary to perform their intended functions. By following this principle, organizations can reduce the attack surface and limit the potential damage that can be caused by compromised accounts or systems.

Web application security is not solely about preventing external threats but also involves monitoring and logging activities within the application. Comprehensive logging and auditing mechanisms help organizations detect and investigate security incidents, track user activities, and gain insights into potential vulnerabilities. Log analysis and real-time monitoring are essential for identifying and responding to security events promptly.

The concept of vulnerability management encompasses the processes of identifying, assessing, and mitigating vulnerabilities within web applications. Vulnerability management programs involve regular vulnerability scanning, penetration testing, and the application of patches and updates to address known vulnerabilities. Timely vulnerability management is critical to reducing the window of opportunity for attackers to exploit weaknesses in web applications.

Security awareness and training are fundamental components of a robust web application security strategy. All individuals involved in the development, maintenance, and operation of web applications must be educated about security best practices and potential threats. Training programs should equip developers, administrators, and other stakeholders with the knowledge and skills needed to identify and mitigate security risks effectively.

The concept of the security development lifecycle (SDLC) emphasizes the integration of security practices throughout the entire software development process. Instead of treating security as an afterthought, organizations following the SDLC approach incorporate security considerations into each phase of the development lifecycle. This proactive approach helps identify and address security issues early, reducing the cost and complexity of remediation later in the development process.

Web application firewalls (WAFs) are security devices or services that filter and monitor incoming web traffic to protect against common web application attacks. By analyzing traffic patterns and applying predefined security rules, WAFs can block malicious requests and help mitigate the risk of web application vulnerabilities being exploited. However, it is essential to configure and maintain WAFs correctly to ensure they provide effective protection.

One of the most crucial concepts in web application security is the principle of continuous improvement. Threats and vulnerabilities evolve over time, and attackers constantly adapt their tactics. To stay ahead of emerging threats, organizations must commit to continuous monitoring, assessment, and improvement of their web application security measures. Regular security updates, vulnerability assessments, and incident response planning are integral parts of this ongoing process.

In summary, these key concepts in web application security form the foundation upon which organizations can build robust defenses against a wide range of threats and vulnerabilities. Implementing these principles, adopting best practices, and staying informed about emerging security trends are essential for protecting web applications and the sensitive data they handle. As the digital landscape continues to evolve, organizations must remain vigilant and proactive in their efforts to secure their web applications effectively.

Chapter 2: Understanding the OWASP Top 10

An overview of the OWASP Top 10 is essential for understanding the most critical web application security risks. The OWASP Top 10 is a well-recognized framework that highlights the top ten vulnerabilities that pose the most significant threats to web applications. Created by the Open Web Application Security Project (OWASP), this list serves as a valuable reference for security professionals, developers, and organizations seeking to prioritize their security efforts effectively.

The primary purpose of the OWASP Top 10 is to raise awareness about common web application vulnerabilities and provide guidance on how to mitigate them. Each vulnerability on the list represents a particular type of threat that web applications may face, and understanding these threats is crucial for building secure web applications. While the OWASP Top 10 is not an exhaustive list of all possible vulnerabilities, it focuses on the vulnerabilities that are most commonly exploited by attackers.

The OWASP Top 10 is updated periodically to reflect the changing threat landscape and the emergence of new vulnerabilities. This ensures that it remains a relevant and up-to-date resource for the security community. Security professionals and organizations should always refer to the latest version of the OWASP Top 10 to stay informed about the most current security risks.

The first vulnerability in the OWASP Top 10 is Injection Attacks. Injection attacks occur when untrusted data is inserted into a web application's input and executed as a command or query. This can lead to various types of attacks, including SQL injection, NoSQL injection, and command injection. Injection attacks are prevalent and can result in data breaches and unauthorized access to sensitive information.

The second vulnerability is Broken Authentication and Session Management. Weak or improper authentication and session management can allow attackers to gain unauthorized access to user accounts or take over user sessions. This vulnerability can lead to identity theft and unauthorized actions on behalf of legitimate users.

Cross-Site Scripting (XSS) is the third vulnerability on the list. XSS vulnerabilities occur when untrusted data is included in a web page and executed in the user's browser. Attackers can use XSS to steal user credentials, inject malicious scripts, and compromise the security of web applications and their users.

The fourth vulnerability is Insecure Direct Object References (IDOR). IDOR vulnerabilities arise when an attacker can manipulate references to objects and access unauthorized data or functionality. This can lead to data exposure and improper access control, compromising the confidentiality and integrity of web applications.

Security Misconfiguration is the fifth vulnerability in the OWASP Top 10. Security misconfigurations occur when web applications, servers, or databases are not properly configured, leaving them vulnerable to exploitation. Attackers can leverage misconfigurations to gain unauthorized access and compromise the security of web applications.

Cross-Site Request Forgery (CSRF) is the sixth vulnerability on the list. CSRF attacks involve tricking users into performing unintended actions on web applications without their consent. Attackers can use CSRF to perform actions on behalf of authenticated users, potentially leading to data manipulation and unauthorized transactions.

The seventh vulnerability is Using Components with Known Vulnerabilities. This vulnerability occurs when web applications use third-party components, libraries, or frameworks that have known security vulnerabilities. Attackers can exploit these vulnerabilities to compromise the security of web applications and their users.

The eighth vulnerability in the OWASP Top 10 is Insufficient Logging and Monitoring. Inadequate logging and monitoring can hinder an organization's ability to detect and respond to security incidents. Without proper visibility into system activities, organizations may not identify and mitigate security threats effectively.

The ninth vulnerability is Insecure Deserialization. Insecure deserialization vulnerabilities can lead to remote code execution and other security risks. Attackers can exploit these vulnerabilities to execute arbitrary code, potentially compromising the security of web applications and their underlying systems.

Unvalidated Redirects and Forwards is the tenth and final vulnerability on the OWASP Top 10 list. This vulnerability occurs when web applications redirect or forward user inputs without proper validation. Attackers can manipulate these redirects to perform phishing attacks or direct users to malicious websites.

It is essential to note that the OWASP Top 10 is not a ranking of vulnerabilities by severity but a list of the most prevalent and impactful security risks. The order of the vulnerabilities may vary depending on the specific context and the security posture of a web application. Organizations should assess their unique risks and prioritize security measures accordingly.

In summary, the OWASP Top 10 provides a comprehensive overview of the most critical web application security vulnerabilities. Understanding these vulnerabilities is the first step in building secure web applications and protecting sensitive data from potential threats. By addressing these vulnerabilities proactively and staying informed about emerging security risks, organizations can enhance their web application security and reduce the risk of security breaches and data compromises.

Common web application vulnerabilities pose significant risks to the security of online systems and the data they process. These vulnerabilities are often exploited by attackers to gain unauthorized access, steal sensitive information, or compromise the functionality of web applications. Understanding these vulnerabilities is essential for developers, security professionals, and organizations striving to protect their web applications and their users.

One of the most prevalent web application vulnerabilities is SQL Injection. SQL Injection occurs when malicious SQL queries are injected into input fields or parameters, allowing attackers to manipulate databases and retrieve, modify, or delete data. This vulnerability arises from improper input validation and inadequate security measures.

Cross-Site Scripting (XSS) is another common web application vulnerability. XSS vulnerabilities enable attackers to inject malicious scripts into web pages that are subsequently executed by unsuspecting users' browsers. These scripts can steal user information, such as cookies or session tokens, and lead to session hijacking or data theft.

Broken Authentication and Session Management is a critical vulnerability that arises from weak or improperly implemented authentication and session management mechanisms. Attackers can exploit this weakness to gain unauthorized access to user accounts or take over legitimate user sessions, potentially compromising sensitive data.

Insecure Direct Object References (IDOR) are vulnerabilities that allow attackers to manipulate references to objects, such as files, databases, or user accounts, to access unauthorized data or perform unauthorized actions. This can lead to data exposure and improper access control.

Security Misconfigurations are widespread web application vulnerabilities resulting from poor configuration settings on web servers, databases, and other components. Attackers can leverage security misconfigurations to gain unauthorized access to systems or data.

Cross-Site Request Forgery (CSRF) vulnerabilities occur when attackers trick users into performing unintended actions on web applications without their consent. CSRF attacks can lead to unauthorized actions, such as changing settings, making financial transactions, or altering user data.

Using Components with Known Vulnerabilities is a vulnerability that arises when web applications incorporate third-party components, libraries, or frameworks with known security flaws. Attackers can exploit these vulnerabilities to compromise the security of web applications and their users.

Inadequate Logging and Monitoring is a vulnerability related to the lack of proper logging and monitoring mechanisms in web applications. Inadequate visibility into system activities hinders the detection and response to security incidents, making it easier for attackers to go unnoticed.

Insecure Deserialization is a web application vulnerability where malicious data is deserialized, potentially leading to remote code execution and other security risks. Attackers can exploit insecure deserialization to execute arbitrary code, compromising the security of web applications and underlying systems.

Unvalidated Redirects and Forwards is a vulnerability that allows attackers to manipulate and redirect user inputs without proper validation. Attackers can use these redirects for phishing attacks or to direct users to malicious websites.

These common web application vulnerabilities highlight the importance of proactive security measures in web development and maintenance. Developers should implement secure coding practices, such as input validation and output encoding, to prevent SQL Injection, XSS, and other injection attacks. Robust authentication and session management mechanisms should be in place to mitigate Broken Authentication and Session Management vulnerabilities.

To address Insecure Direct Object References, developers should implement proper access controls and validation checks for user inputs. Security misconfigurations can be mitigated through proper configuration management and regular security assessments. CSRF protection mechanisms should be in place to prevent Cross-Site Request Forgery attacks.

To address the use of components with known vulnerabilities, organizations should maintain an up-to-date inventory of third-party components and promptly apply patches and updates when security flaws are discovered. Inadequate logging and monitoring can be addressed by implementing comprehensive logging and real-time monitoring solutions to detect and respond to security incidents effectively.

Insecure deserialization vulnerabilities can be mitigated by following secure deserialization practices and avoiding the use of insecure serialization formats. Proper validation and encoding of user inputs can prevent Unvalidated Redirects and Forwards, ensuring that user inputs are safe and do not lead to unintended actions.

It is important to note that web application vulnerabilities are not static; they evolve over time as attackers develop new techniques and as technologies change. Security professionals and organizations must remain vigilant, staying informed about emerging threats and best practices to protect against them.

Moreover, addressing web application vulnerabilities requires a holistic approach that encompasses secure coding, regular security testing, and ongoing monitoring and response. Organizations should implement security as a fundamental aspect of their development and operational processes, involving developers, administrators, and other stakeholders in the effort to protect web applications and the sensitive data they handle.

In summary, understanding common web application vulnerabilities is essential for building and maintaining secure web applications. These vulnerabilities can have severe consequences, including data breaches, financial losses, and damage to an organization's reputation. By addressing these vulnerabilities proactively and adopting a security-first mindset, organizations can reduce the risk of security incidents and provide a safer online experience for their users.

Top of Form

Chapter 3: Injection Attacks: The Silent Killers

Injection attacks are a prevalent and critical type of web application vulnerability. They involve the malicious injection of untrusted data or code into an application's inputs, with the intent of manipulating or compromising the application's behavior. Injection attacks can target various aspects of an application, including databases, web servers, operating systems, and more. These attacks are not limited to a single programming language or technology; they can affect any application that processes user inputs without proper validation and sanitization.

One of the most well-known and common types of injection attacks is SQL Injection. SQL Injection occurs when an attacker injects malicious SQL queries into user inputs that interact with a database. This can lead to unauthorized access to the database, retrieval of sensitive information, modification of data, and even complete database compromise. SQL Injection attacks can have devastating consequences, as they can result in data breaches and data manipulation.

Another form of injection attack is NoSQL Injection, which targets NoSQL databases. In NoSQL databases, data is often stored in a schema-less format, making it challenging to perform traditional SQL Injection attacks. However, attackers can still exploit vulnerabilities by injecting malicious queries or data that disrupt the database's operations or compromise data integrity.

Command Injection is yet another type of injection attack that focuses on executing malicious commands on the underlying operating system. Attackers inject specially crafted input that the application unintentionally passes to the operating system as a command. Successful command injection can allow attackers to take control of the host system, execute arbitrary commands, and potentially compromise the entire server.

Cross-Site Scripting (XSS) is a type of injection attack that targets web applications by injecting malicious scripts into web pages viewed by other users. In an XSS attack, attackers inject script code into the application's input fields or parameters, which is then executed by other users' browsers. This can lead to session hijacking, data theft, and the spread of malware.

In addition to SQL Injection, NoSQL Injection, Command Injection, and XSS, there are other injection attacks that target specific technologies and platforms. For example, LDAP Injection targets applications that use LDAP (Lightweight Directory Access Protocol) for authentication and directory services. XML Injection focuses on injecting malicious XML content into XML-based applications, potentially leading to data exposure and application compromise.

Injection attacks are often made possible by inadequate input validation and insufficient output encoding. Input validation involves checking and filtering user inputs to ensure they conform to expected formats and are free from malicious content. Output encoding involves encoding data before rendering it to the user's browser, preventing malicious code execution.

Preventing injection attacks requires a multi-layered approach to security. Secure coding practices are fundamental in preventing these attacks. Developers should implement parameterized queries, prepared statements, and stored procedures to mitigate SQL Injection. For NoSQL Injection, developers should validate and sanitize input before interacting with NoSQL databases.

To prevent Command Injection, applications should avoid using user inputs directly in system commands and should validate and sanitize inputs properly. For XSS prevention, output encoding and input validation are crucial, along with implementing security headers like Content Security Policy (CSP) to restrict the execution of scripts.

Regular security testing and code reviews can help identify and address injection vulnerabilities. Automated security tools and manual testing by security professionals can uncover potential weaknesses that need remediation.

Web application firewalls (WAFs) are also effective in detecting and blocking injection attacks by analyzing incoming traffic and applying security rules to filter out malicious input. However, relying solely on a WAF is not a comprehensive solution, as it may not catch all injection attacks, and attackers may find ways to bypass it.

In summary, injection attacks are a persistent and significant threat to web applications and systems. They exploit vulnerabilities in the way applications handle user inputs, allowing attackers to manipulate or compromise the application's behavior. Preventing injection attacks requires a combination of secure coding practices, input validation, output encoding, regular security testing, and the use of security tools like web application firewalls. By proactively addressing injection vulnerabilities, organizations can enhance the security of their web applications and protect sensitive data from potential threats.

Injection attacks encompass a variety of attack techniques that exploit vulnerabilities in software systems, allowing attackers to inject malicious code or data into an application's inputs or parameters. These attacks are a prevalent and critical security concern, as they can lead to data breaches, unauthorized access, and the compromise of entire systems. Understanding the different types of injection attacks is essential for developing effective security measures and protecting against these threats.

One of the most well-known injection attacks is SQL Injection, which targets applications that interact with relational databases. In SQL Injection attacks, attackers inject malicious SQL queries into user inputs, exploiting vulnerabilities in the application's input handling. Successful SQL Injection attacks can enable attackers to retrieve, modify, or delete data from the database, potentially leading to data breaches and unauthorized access.

NoSQL Injection is a variant of injection attacks that focuses on NoSQL databases, which are commonly used for handling unstructured or semi-structured data. Attackers exploit vulnerabilities in applications interacting with NoSQL databases by injecting malicious queries or data, which can disrupt the database's operations or compromise data integrity.

Command Injection attacks aim to execute malicious commands on the underlying operating system. These attacks occur when an attacker injects specially crafted input into an application's parameters, and the application unintentionally passes this input to the operating system as a command. Successful command injection can allow attackers to take control of the host system, execute arbitrary commands, and potentially compromise the entire server.

Cross-Site Scripting (XSS) is another injection attack that targets web applications by injecting malicious scripts into web pages viewed by other users. In XSS attacks, attackers inject script code into input fields or parameters, which is then executed by the browsers of other users who visit the compromised web page. This can lead to session hijacking, data theft, and the spread of malware.

LDAP Injection is a type of injection attack that targets applications using the Lightweight Directory Access Protocol (LDAP) for authentication and directory services. Attackers manipulate input data to inject malicious LDAP queries, potentially gaining unauthorized access or retrieving sensitive information from directory services.

XML Injection attacks focus on injecting malicious XML content into XML-based applications. Attackers exploit vulnerabilities in applications processing XML inputs by injecting malicious XML data that can disrupt the application's functionality, expose sensitive data, or lead to application compromise.

Similarly, XPath Injection attacks target applications that use XPath (XML Path Language) for querying XML data. Attackers inject malicious XPath expressions into user inputs, potentially gaining unauthorized access or extracting sensitive information from XML documents.

In addition to these common injection attacks, there are other specialized injection attacks that target specific technologies and platforms. For example, Object-Relational Mapping (ORM) Injection attacks exploit vulnerabilities in applications using ORM frameworks to interact with databases, while Template Injection attacks target applications that use template engines for rendering dynamic content.

Preventing injection attacks requires a multi-layered approach to security. Secure coding practices are fundamental in preventing these attacks. Developers should implement parameterized queries, prepared statements, and stored procedures to mitigate SQL Injection. For NoSQL Injection, developers should validate and sanitize input before interacting with NoSQL databases.

To prevent Command Injection, applications should avoid using user inputs directly in system commands and should validate and sanitize inputs properly. For XSS prevention, output encoding and input validation are crucial, along with implementing security headers like Content Security Policy (CSP) to restrict the execution of scripts.

Regular security testing and code reviews can help identify and address injection vulnerabilities. Automated security tools and manual testing by security professionals can uncover potential weaknesses that need remediation.

Web application firewalls (WAFs) are also effective in detecting and blocking injection attacks by analyzing incoming traffic and applying security rules to filter out malicious input. However, relying solely on a WAF is not a comprehensive solution, as it may not catch all injection attacks, and attackers may find ways to bypass it.

In summary, injection attacks are a persistent and significant threat to web applications and systems. They exploit vulnerabilities in the way applications handle user inputs, allowing attackers to manipulate or compromise the application's behavior. Preventing injection attacks requires a combination of secure coding practices, input validation, output encoding, regular security testing, and the use of security tools like web application firewalls. By proactively addressing injection vulnerabilities, organizations can enhance the security of their web applications and protect sensitive data from potential threats.

Chapter 4: Broken Authentication and Session Management

Authentication is a fundamental aspect of information security that plays a critical role in verifying the identities of users and entities seeking access to systems, applications, and resources. It is the process by which individuals, devices, or services prove their identity to an authentication system, establishing trust and enabling secure interactions in the digital world. The importance of authentication cannot be overstated, as it serves as a foundational element in safeguarding data, protecting privacy, and preventing unauthorized access to sensitive information.

In today's interconnected and digitalized environment, where virtually every aspect of our lives relies on technology and online services, authentication is paramount. Users must be able to access their email accounts, social media profiles, banking applications, and other online services securely and confidently. Without robust authentication mechanisms in place, these services would be vulnerable to unauthorized access, data breaches, and identity theft.

Authentication is essential in ensuring that individuals have the appropriate level of access to systems and resources. For example, in an organization, employees need to access specific files, applications, and databases based on their roles and responsibilities. Proper authentication helps enforce access control policies, ensuring that users can only access the resources they are authorized to use.

Authentication is also integral to protecting sensitive data, such as personal information, financial records, and medical records. In healthcare, for instance, healthcare providers must authenticate themselves to access patient records, ensuring that only authorized personnel can view and update this sensitive information. Without authentication, patient privacy would be compromised, and the integrity of healthcare data would be at risk.

Furthermore, authentication plays a crucial role in e-commerce and online transactions. When individuals make online purchases or conduct financial transactions, they need assurance that their financial information and payment details are secure. Authentication mechanisms, such as two-factor authentication (2FA) and biometric authentication, provide an extra layer of security to confirm the identity of users before allowing them to complete transactions.

Authentication not only benefits users but also organizations and service providers. Robust authentication mechanisms can help protect businesses from fraud, unauthorized access, and data breaches, thereby safeguarding their reputation and financial interests. Organizations that fail to implement adequate authentication measures may face legal and regulatory consequences for failing to protect sensitive customer data.

There are various methods and factors used in authentication processes to establish identity and grant access. These methods include something the user knows (such as a password or PIN), something the user has (such as a smart card or security token), and something the user is (biometric characteristics like fingerprints or facial recognition). Multifactor authentication (MFA) combines two or more of these factors to enhance security further.

The choice of authentication method depends on the level of security required and the specific use case. In high-security environments, organizations may implement advanced authentication methods, such as biometrics, to ensure the identity of users. In contrast, for less critical applications, a simple username and password may suffice.

Despite the critical importance of authentication, it is not without its challenges and vulnerabilities. One of the primary challenges is the management of passwords. Users often struggle to create and remember strong, unique passwords for each online service they use. This leads to the use of weak passwords, password reuse across multiple accounts, and the risk of password-related attacks like brute force and credential stuffing.

Phishing attacks are another significant challenge in the realm of authentication. Attackers use deceptive emails or websites to trick users into divulging their login credentials. Even individuals who are generally cautious can fall victim to well-crafted phishing campaigns, highlighting the need for user education and awareness.

In response to these challenges, organizations and service providers are adopting more secure authentication methods and practices. Two-factor authentication (2FA) and multi-factor authentication (MFA) have gained popularity as they add an additional layer of security beyond passwords. These methods often require users to provide something they know (password) and something they have (a temporary code from a mobile app or a hardware token).

Biometric authentication is also becoming increasingly prevalent, with devices like smartphones and laptops equipped with fingerprint sensors and facial recognition technology. Biometrics offer a convenient and secure way to authenticate users based on unique physical characteristics, making it challenging for attackers to impersonate someone else.

Additionally, the use of single sign-on (SSO) solutions allows users to access multiple applications and services with a single set of credentials. SSO simplifies the authentication process while enhancing security by reducing the number of passwords users need to manage.

In summary, authentication is a cornerstone of information security, serving as the gatekeeper that verifies the identity of users and entities seeking access to digital systems and resources. Its importance extends to protecting data, safeguarding privacy, and preventing unauthorized access to sensitive information. As technology continues to evolve, so do authentication methods, with organizations and service providers adopting more secure and convenient authentication solutions to address the challenges and vulnerabilities of traditional username and password-based authentication. By recognizing the significance of authentication and implementing appropriate security measures, individuals and organizations can navigate the digital world with greater confidence and security.

Secure session management is a crucial aspect of web application security that plays a vital role in protecting user data, ensuring privacy, and preventing unauthorized access. Sessions are temporary interactions between a user and a web application, initiated when a user logs in and terminated when the user logs out or becomes inactive. Properly managing sessions is essential for maintaining the confidentiality and integrity of user data throughout their interactions with the application.

Session management involves several key practices and considerations to ensure security:

Unique Session Identifiers: Each session should have a unique identifier or token associated with it. This identifier is used to link a user's actions and data during their session and should be sufficiently random and unpredictable to prevent session fixation attacks.

Session Timeout: Implementing session timeouts is critical to ensure that inactive sessions are automatically terminated after a predefined period. This reduces the risk of unauthorized access if a user leaves their session unattended.

Secure Session Storage: Session data should be stored securely on the server-side, and sensitive information should never be stored in cookies or on the client-side. This prevents attackers from tampering with or stealing session data.

Strong Session Management Algorithms: Use strong cryptographic algorithms and best practices for generating session identifiers and protecting session data. This includes using secure random number generators and encryption to secure session data.

Session Data Validation: Validate and sanitize session data to prevent injection attacks and other security vulnerabilities. Ensure that data received from the client is consistent with expected formats and ranges.

Logout Functionality: Provide users with a clear and effective way to log out of their sessions. Logging out should invalidate the session identifier and clear any associated session data.

Protection Against Session Fixation: Implement measures to protect against session fixation attacks, where an attacker sets a user's session identifier. Techniques like session regeneration or associating sessions with client IP addresses can help mitigate this risk.

Cross-Site Request Forgery (CSRF) Protection: Protect against CSRF attacks by implementing anti-CSRF tokens and validating incoming requests. CSRF attacks can trick users into performing unwanted actions while authenticated.

Secure Transport Layer: Ensure that sessions are established and maintained over a secure transport layer using protocols like HTTPS. This prevents eavesdropping and man-in-the-middle attacks on session data.

Session Expiry Handling: Handle session expiry gracefully by notifying users and offering them the option to reauthenticate when their session expires. Avoid displaying sensitive information in error messages.

Session Revocation: Implement mechanisms to revoke or invalidate sessions when a user's account is compromised or when a user requests it. This is especially important for user privacy and security.

Monitoring and Logging: Implement comprehensive session monitoring and logging to detect and respond to suspicious activities or unauthorized access attempts. Monitor for unusual patterns, such as multiple login failures.

Security Headers: Use security headers like HttpOnly and Secure flags for cookies to enhance session security. HttpOnly prevents JavaScript access to cookies, and Secure ensures cookies are only transmitted over HTTPS.

User Education: Educate users about the importance of secure session management practices. Encourage them to log out from shared or public computers and to use strong, unique passwords.

Third-Party Services: Be cautious when integrating third-party services or components that handle session management. Ensure that these services follow secure session management practices and meet your security requirements.

Regular Security Testing: Perform regular security testing, including penetration testing and vulnerability assessments, to identify and address any session management vulnerabilities. Test the application's ability to handle various session-related attacks.

In summary, secure session management is a critical component of web application security that helps protect user data, privacy, and the overall integrity of an application. By implementing secure session management practices, organizations can reduce the risk of session-related vulnerabilities, unauthorized access, and data breaches. It is essential to stay updated with the latest security best practices and continually assess and enhance session management security to adapt to evolving threats and vulnerabilities in the digital landscape.

Chapter 5: Cross-Site Scripting (XSS) Demystified

Cross-Site Scripting, commonly abbreviated as XSS, is a prevalent and potentially dangerous web application vulnerability that allows attackers to inject malicious scripts into web pages viewed by other users. This type of attack targets the trust users place in a website, as the malicious script appears to be a legitimate part of the web application. XSS attacks can have serious consequences, including the theft of sensitive data, session hijacking, and the spread of malware to unsuspecting users. Understanding XSS is essential for developers, security professionals, and website owners to protect their applications and users from this pervasive threat.

XSS attacks occur when an attacker injects malicious script code into web pages, which is then executed by the browsers of other users who visit those pages. This script code can be written in various programming languages, including JavaScript, and can perform a wide range of actions, depending on the attacker's intentions. XSS attacks are typically divided into three main categories: Stored XSS, Reflected XSS, and DOM-based XSS. Each category has distinct characteristics and impacts, but all involve the injection of malicious scripts into web pages.

Stored XSS attacks occur when the injected malicious script is permanently stored on the target website and is presented to other users whenever they access the compromised page. This type of attack can have a long-lasting impact as the script continues to execute whenever users view the infected page, potentially leading to data theft, account compromise, and other malicious activities.

Reflected XSS attacks involve the injection of malicious script code into a URL or a web form, which is then reflected back to the user as part of the response from the web server. The user's browser then executes the script code within the context of the visited website. Reflected XSS attacks are typically short-lived and rely on tricking users into clicking on malicious links or submitting malicious forms.

DOM-based XSS attacks, on the other hand, manipulate the Document Object Model (DOM) of a web page to execute malicious code. This type of attack is more complex and challenging to detect, as it doesn't necessarily involve server-side vulnerabilities. Instead, it relies on manipulating the client-side code and behaviors of a web application.

The impact of XSS attacks can be severe. Attackers can steal user cookies, session tokens, or other sensitive information, allowing them to impersonate users and gain unauthorized access to their accounts. They can also deface websites, redirect users to malicious websites, or initiate actions on behalf of the user without their consent. Furthermore, when attackers inject malicious scripts that spread malware, they can compromise the security of users' devices and compromise their data.

To prevent XSS attacks, it is essential to implement secure coding practices and employ security mechanisms within web applications. Some key preventive measures include:

Input Validation: Validate and sanitize user inputs to ensure they conform to expected formats and do not contain malicious code. Proper input validation helps prevent attackers from injecting scripts into web forms and URLs.

Output Encoding: Encode data before rendering it to a web page to ensure that any user-generated content is treated as plain text and not executed as script code.

Content Security Policy (CSP): Implement CSP headers in web applications to define which scripts can be executed, mitigating the impact of XSS attacks. CSP restricts the sources from which scripts can be loaded, reducing the risk of executing malicious code.

Escape Special Characters: Escape characters that have special meanings in HTML, JavaScript, and other scripting languages to prevent them from being interpreted as code.

HttpOnly and Secure Flags: Set the HttpOnly flag on cookies to prevent JavaScript access to cookies, and use the Secure flag to ensure cookies are transmitted only over secure connections.

Regular Security Testing: Conduct security testing, including automated scanning and manual code reviews, to identify and remediate vulnerabilities in web applications.

Security Awareness Training: Educate developers, administrators, and users about the risks and prevention of XSS attacks. Promote a security-aware culture within organizations to minimize the likelihood of successful attacks.

In summary, Cross-Site Scripting (XSS) is a prevalent and dangerous web application vulnerability that can have serious consequences for both users and website owners. Understanding the different types of XSS attacks and implementing robust security measures is essential for mitigating this threat. By following secure coding practices, implementing security headers like Content

Security Policy (CSP), and conducting regular security testing, organizations can significantly reduce the risk of XSS attacks and provide a safer online experience for their users.

Chapter 6: Insecure Direct Object References

Insecure Direct Object Reference (IDOR) is a critical web application security vulnerability that arises when an application provides improper access controls to objects or resources based on user-supplied input. This vulnerability occurs when an attacker can manipulate input parameters, such as URLs or form fields, to access unauthorized data or functionality within the application. IDOR vulnerabilities can have severe consequences, including unauthorized data disclosure, account takeover, and data manipulation.

To understand IDOR, it's essential to grasp the concept of direct object references. A direct object reference occurs when an application exposes internal implementation objects, such as files or database records, directly to users without proper validation or authorization checks. In other words, instead of enforcing strict access controls, the application relies on user inputs (often in the form of identifiers) to determine which resources to access.

For example, consider a web application that manages user profiles, where each user's profile is identified by a unique numeric identifier. To view their profile, users typically access a URL like **https://example.com/profile?id=123**. In this case, the numeric value "123" is used as an identifier to retrieve the corresponding user's profile.

The problem arises when the application fails to verify whether the user making the request has the legitimate authority to access that particular resource. Insecure

Direct Object Reference occurs when an attacker modifies the identifier in the URL, such as changing it to **https://example.com/profile?id=456**, to access another user's profile, which they are not authorized to view.

The impact of IDOR vulnerabilities can vary depending on the context and the specific resources accessible. In some cases, attackers can access sensitive user data, including personal information, financial records, or private messages. In other instances, IDOR can allow attackers to perform unauthorized actions, such as changing other users' settings or deleting their data.

Mitigating Insecure Direct Object Reference vulnerabilities requires a combination of secure coding practices and proper access controls. Here are some essential steps to prevent and address IDOR:

Access Controls: Implement strict access controls and authorization mechanisms in your application to ensure that users can only access resources they are authorized to view or modify. Never rely solely on user-supplied input to determine access rights.

Use Indirect References: Avoid exposing internal identifiers directly to users. Instead, use indirect references or tokens that are meaningless to attackers and do not correspond directly to sensitive resources.

Session-based Access: Tie resource access to authenticated user sessions rather than using user-supplied input as the sole determinant of access rights. Ensure that session management is secure to prevent session fixation and hijacking.

Validation and Whitelisting: Validate and sanitize user inputs rigorously to prevent manipulation. Use whitelisting approaches to define valid input values, and reject any requests that do not conform to these whitelists.

Unique Identifiers: Generate unique, unpredictable identifiers for resources, such as using universally unique identifiers (UUIDs) or other methods that make it extremely difficult for attackers to guess or manipulate identifiers.

Testing and Code Review: Conduct regular security testing, including penetration testing and code reviews, to identify and address IDOR vulnerabilities in your application. Ensure that testers and reviewers attempt to access resources they shouldn't have access to.

Automated Scanning: Employ automated security scanning tools to identify potential IDOR vulnerabilities. These tools can help detect weaknesses that may be missed during manual testing.

Logging and Monitoring: Implement comprehensive logging and monitoring to track access to sensitive resources. Regularly review logs for suspicious or unauthorized activities and respond promptly to any anomalies.

Incident Response: Develop an incident response plan that includes procedures for handling potential IDOR incidents. Be prepared to investigate, mitigate, and notify affected users if a vulnerability is exploited.

In summary, Insecure Direct Object Reference (IDOR) is a significant web application security vulnerability that can result in unauthorized access to sensitive resources and data. Understanding the concept of direct object references and implementing proper access controls is essential to mitigate IDOR vulnerabilities effectively. By following secure coding practices, conducting regular testing, and staying vigilant for potential IDOR weaknesses, organizations can enhance the security of their web applications and protect user data from unauthorized access and manipulation.

Securing direct object references is a critical aspect of web application security that focuses on preventing Insecure Direct Object Reference (IDOR) vulnerabilities. Direct object references occur when an application exposes internal objects or resources directly to users without adequate access controls or validation. These vulnerabilities can lead to unauthorized access to sensitive data or functionality, potentially resulting in data breaches and security incidents.

Securing direct object references begins with a robust access control system. Access controls should be implemented throughout the application to ensure that users can only access resources they are authorized to view or manipulate. This involves verifying user permissions and comparing them to the requested resource.

One essential principle in securing direct object references is to avoid exposing internal implementation details to users. Identifiers or references used to access resources should be meaningless to attackers and not directly correspond to the internal structure of the application. This makes it more challenging for attackers to manipulate or guess resource identifiers.

For example, instead of using sequential numeric IDs for database records in URLs, it's better to use universally unique identifiers (UUIDs) or other randomized identifiers that are not predictable. This helps prevent attackers from easily enumerating and accessing resources.

Implementing session-based access controls is another key practice. Resource access should be tied to authenticated user sessions, ensuring that only authorized users with valid session tokens can access specific resources. This approach helps prevent session fixation and hijacking, which are common attack vectors in IDOR vulnerabilities.

Validation and whitelisting play crucial roles in securing direct object references. User inputs, such as resource identifiers or references, should be rigorously validated and sanitized. Whitelisting involves defining a list of valid input values and rejecting any requests that do not conform to these predefined values. By using whitelists, developers can reduce the risk of attackers manipulating input data.

Unique resource identifiers should be generated for each resource. These identifiers should be unpredictable and challenging for attackers to guess. By using unique identifiers, even if an attacker discovers one resource's identifier, it won't provide them with a template to access other resources.

Security testing is an essential part of securing direct object references. Regular security testing, including penetration testing and code reviews, should be conducted to identify and address any potential vulnerabilities in the application. Testers should attempt to access resources they shouldn't have access to, simulating real-world attack scenarios.

Automated security scanning tools can complement manual testing efforts. These tools can help detect potential direct object reference vulnerabilities by analyzing the application's code and behavior. While automated tools are valuable, they should not replace manual testing and code review processes.

Logging and monitoring are crucial for securing direct object references. Comprehensive logging should be in place to record all access attempts to sensitive resources. Monitoring systems should regularly review logs for suspicious or unauthorized activities, allowing security teams to respond promptly to any anomalies.

An incident response plan is an essential component of securing direct object references. Organizations should have procedures in place for handling potential IDOR incidents. These procedures should include investigation, mitigation, and notification of affected users if a vulnerability is exploited.

It's important to consider the role of error handling in securing direct object references. Error messages should not reveal sensitive information about the application's internal structure or resource identifiers. Error messages should be generic and not provide clues to attackers about the resources they are trying to access.

Security awareness training is valuable for all stakeholders involved in the development and operation of web applications. Developers, administrators, and even end-users should be educated about the risks associated with direct object references and best practices for secure usage.

Security frameworks and libraries that include built-in direct object reference protection mechanisms can be advantageous. These tools can automate some of the security practices, such as output encoding and access controls, reducing the likelihood of vulnerabilities.

Regularly updating and patching web application components is essential for securing direct object references. Outdated libraries, plugins, and frameworks may contain known vulnerabilities that attackers can exploit. By keeping all components up to date, organizations can reduce the attack surface and minimize the risk of direct object reference vulnerabilities.

In summary, securing direct object references is crucial for preventing Insecure Direct Object Reference (IDOR) vulnerabilities in web applications. This involves implementing robust access controls, avoiding the exposure of internal details, and tying resource access to authenticated user sessions. Validation, whitelisting, and unique resource identifiers are essential practices, and security testing, monitoring, and incident response play critical roles in the overall security strategy. By following these practices and promoting security awareness throughout the organization, web application developers and administrators can enhance security and protect sensitive data from unauthorized access and manipulation.

Chapter 7: Security Misconfiguration: A Common Pitfall

Security misconfiguration is a common and potentially severe security risk that can have significant consequences for organizations and their web applications. This risk arises when security settings, configurations, or defaults are improperly set, leaving vulnerabilities exposed and potentially exploitable by attackers. Security misconfigurations can occur at various levels, including the operating system, web server, application server, database, and application code.

One of the most prevalent forms of security misconfiguration is exposed sensitive information. This can include passwords, API keys, database connection strings, and other sensitive data that should be protected. When such information is inadvertently exposed, it can provide attackers with the means to access systems or data they shouldn't have access to.

Another common security misconfiguration involves overly permissive access controls. When access controls are not properly configured, attackers may gain unauthorized access to resources or functionality within an application. For example, if a file directory is left with public read and write permissions, anyone can access and modify files stored there.

Insecure default settings are a significant source of security misconfigurations. Many software packages and frameworks come with default configurations that are not optimized for security. If administrators do not review and modify these settings, they may inadvertently expose vulnerabilities.

Failure to apply security patches and updates promptly is another form of security misconfiguration. Software vendors regularly release patches to fix known vulnerabilities, and failing to apply these updates leaves systems exposed to known exploits. Attackers actively search for unpatched systems to exploit.

Inadequate error handling and verbose error messages can also lead to security misconfigurations. Detailed error messages can reveal sensitive information about the system's architecture, which attackers can use to exploit vulnerabilities. Developers should ensure that error messages are generic and do not provide attackers with clues about the system's internals.

Excessive permissions and unnecessary functionality can result from security misconfigurations. If an application or user account has more privileges than necessary, it increases the attack surface and the potential impact of a successful attack. Regularly reviewing and limiting permissions is essential.

Security misconfigurations can manifest in various ways, depending on the specific components and technologies involved. For example, misconfigurations in a web server might lead to directory traversal attacks, where attackers can access files outside of the webroot. In the case of a database misconfiguration, attackers might exploit open database ports to access and manipulate data.

The consequences of security misconfigurations can be severe. Attackers can steal sensitive data, compromise user accounts, deface websites, and gain unauthorized access to systems. The impact may extend to reputational damage, legal and regulatory consequences, and financial losses.

To mitigate the risks associated with security misconfigurations, organizations should adopt a proactive and comprehensive approach to security.

One fundamental step is conducting regular security assessments, including vulnerability scanning and penetration testing. These assessments help identify and address misconfigurations in a systematic manner.

Implementing secure coding practices is crucial for developers. They should follow best practices, such as validating input, encoding output, and avoiding hardcoded secrets.

Automated security tools and configuration checkers can assist in identifying and correcting misconfigurations. These tools can scan systems for common configuration errors and suggest remediation steps.

Organizations should maintain an inventory of all assets, software, and configurations. This inventory helps ensure that all systems are properly configured and up to date.

Security configurations should be reviewed and updated regularly. This includes reviewing settings for operating systems, web servers, application servers, databases, and application code.

The principle of least privilege should be applied diligently. Users and systems should have only the permissions and access they need to perform their tasks. Excess permissions should be revoked.

Security misconfigurations can be minimized by following industry-specific security guidelines and standards. For example, organizations in the healthcare industry can adhere to the Health Insurance Portability and Accountability Act (HIPAA) security rule, while those in finance can follow Payment Card Industry Data Security Standard (PCI DSS) requirements.

Regularly monitoring system logs and implementing intrusion detection systems can help identify and respond to security misconfigurations and unauthorized access quickly.

Education and awareness training for developers, administrators, and users are essential. Everyone should understand the importance of security configurations and their role in preventing misconfigurations.

An incident response plan should be in place to address security incidents promptly. This plan should include procedures for identifying and remediating misconfigurations and managing the consequences of security breaches.

In summary, security misconfigurations pose significant risks to organizations and their web applications. These risks can lead to unauthorized access, data breaches, and reputational damage. To mitigate these risks, organizations should adopt proactive security practices, conduct regular assessments, and follow industry-specific guidelines. By doing so, they can minimize the likelihood of security misconfigurations and enhance the overall security posture of their systems and applications.

Avoiding security misconfigurations is a critical aspect of maintaining the security of your systems and applications. Security misconfigurations can lead to significant vulnerabilities and expose your organization to various risks. To prevent security misconfigurations effectively, it's important to follow best practices and adopt a proactive security stance.

One of the fundamental steps in avoiding security misconfigurations is to conduct a comprehensive inventory of all your systems, software, and configurations. This inventory will help you gain a clear understanding of your environment and the potential points of misconfiguration. By knowing what you have, you can better manage and secure it.

Implementing the principle of least privilege is crucial. This means granting users, applications, and systems only the permissions and access they need to perform their specific tasks. By minimizing unnecessary privileges, you reduce the attack surface and limit the potential impact of misconfigurations.

Regularly reviewing and updating security configurations is essential. This includes settings for operating systems, web servers, application servers, databases, and application code. Configuration settings can change over time, so it's important to keep them up to date to reflect your organization's evolving security requirements.

Adhering to industry-specific security guidelines and standards is another key practice. Many industries have established security standards that provide specific recommendations and requirements for securing systems and applications. For example, organizations in healthcare can follow the Health Insurance Portability and Accountability Act (HIPAA) security rule, while those in finance can adhere to Payment Card Industry Data Security Standard (PCI DSS) requirements.

Implementing secure coding practices is crucial for developers. They should follow best practices, such as validating input, encoding output, and avoiding hardcoded secrets. Properly trained developers can significantly reduce the risk of security misconfigurations in application code.

Automated security tools and configuration checkers can be invaluable in identifying and mitigating security misconfigurations. These tools can scan systems for common configuration errors and suggest remediation steps. Regularly using such tools as part of your security processes can help catch misconfigurations before they become vulnerabilities.

Regularly monitoring system logs and implementing intrusion detection systems are essential for quickly identifying and responding to security misconfigurations and unauthorized access. Monitoring helps detect anomalies and potential misconfigurations in real time, allowing for prompt remediation.

Education and awareness training for developers, administrators, and users play a critical role in preventing security misconfigurations. Everyone involved in the organization's systems and applications should understand the importance of security configurations and their role in avoiding misconfigurations.

An incident response plan should be in place to address security incidents promptly. This plan should include procedures for identifying and remediating misconfigurations, as well as managing the consequences of security breaches. Having a well-defined plan can minimize the impact of misconfigurations when they occur.

Using security frameworks and libraries that include built-in security features can help mitigate the risk of misconfigurations. These tools often come with predefined secure settings and features that can enhance the overall security posture of your systems and applications.

Security misconfigurations can also be minimized by avoiding the use of default settings whenever possible. Default settings are often not optimized for security and may expose vulnerabilities. It's essential to review and adjust default settings to align them with your organization's security requirements.

Implementing proper error handling and avoiding verbose error messages can prevent attackers from gaining insights into the system's internal structure and potential misconfigurations. Error messages should be generic and not provide attackers with information that could aid in exploiting vulnerabilities.

Regularly applying security patches and updates is crucial. Software vendors release patches to address known vulnerabilities, and failing to apply these updates leaves systems exposed to known exploits. Attackers actively search for unpatched systems to exploit.

Implementing a robust access control system is fundamental in avoiding security misconfigurations. Access controls should be properly configured to ensure that users can only access resources they are authorized to view or modify. Regularly review and adjust access control settings as needed.

Security misconfigurations can manifest in various ways, depending on the specific components and technologies involved. For example, misconfigurations in a web server might lead to directory traversal attacks, where attackers can access files outside of the webroot. In the case of a database misconfiguration, attackers might exploit open database ports to access and manipulate data.

Security misconfigurations can have severe consequences, including unauthorized access, data breaches, reputational damage, legal and regulatory consequences, and financial losses. By adopting a proactive approach to security, regularly reviewing and updating configurations, following best practices, and staying informed about emerging threats, organizations can significantly reduce the risk of security misconfigurations and enhance the overall security of their systems and applications.

Chapter 8: Cross-Site Request Forgery (CSRF) Uncovered

Cross-Site Request Forgery (CSRF) is a web application security vulnerability that can have serious implications for the security and functionality of web applications. At its core, CSRF is an attack that tricks a user's browser into making an unintended and potentially malicious request on behalf of the user. This can result in actions being taken on a user's behalf without their consent or knowledge.

The essence of a CSRF attack lies in its ability to exploit the trust that a web application places in a user's browser. When a user logs into a web application, the application often stores authentication tokens or session cookies in the user's browser to maintain their session. These tokens are used to verify the user's identity and ensure that they have the necessary permissions to perform actions within the application.

In a CSRF attack, an attacker tricks a user into unknowingly making a request to a different website or domain that performs an action on a web application where the user is authenticated. This happens because the user's browser automatically includes any stored authentication tokens or cookies when making requests to the target site, regardless of where the request originates.

For example, suppose a user is logged into their online banking account and visits a malicious website. If the attacker has crafted a CSRF attack on the user's online banking site, the user's browser, without their knowledge, might execute actions like transferring money or changing account details when they visit the malicious site.

The potential consequences of CSRF attacks can be significant. Attackers can use CSRF to manipulate user accounts, change settings, delete data, or even perform financial transactions, all without the user's consent. These attacks can lead to data loss, financial losses, and damage to an organization's reputation.

To defend against CSRF attacks, web applications must implement various security measures. One of the most effective countermeasures is the use of anti-CSRF tokens. These tokens are unique and random values generated by the server and embedded in forms or requests. When a user submits a form or performs an action, the anti-CSRF token must be included and validated by the server to ensure that the request is legitimate and not the result of a CSRF attack.

Another essential mitigation technique is same-site cookies. These cookies are designed to restrict the scope of cookies to the same site from which they originated. By setting the "SameSite" attribute on cookies, web applications can prevent browsers from sending authentication tokens to cross-site requests, making CSRF attacks less effective.

Cross-Origin Resource Sharing (CORS) policies are another defense mechanism against CSRF. CORS policies specify which domains are allowed to make cross-origin requests to a web application. By configuring these policies, web applications can control which sites are permitted to access their resources and perform actions on behalf of users.

Session management practices also play a vital role in CSRF prevention. Web applications should ensure that session tokens are properly protected and that users are authenticated before performing sensitive actions. Additionally, session tokens should have a short lifespan and be renewed regularly to limit their potential exposure. Developers should also avoid placing sensitive actions behind predictable URLs or endpoints. For example, actions like changing a password or initiating a financial transaction should not be accessible through simple, predictable URLs that can be exploited by CSRF attacks. User education is an essential aspect of CSRF prevention. Users should be informed about the risks of clicking on suspicious links or visiting untrusted websites while logged into sensitive accounts. By understanding the potential consequences of CSRF attacks, users can take precautions to safeguard their accounts.

Web application security testing, including vulnerability scanning and penetration testing, should be conducted regularly to identify and address CSRF vulnerabilities. Testing helps ensure that security measures are effective and that potential weaknesses are discovered and remedied.

Incident response plans should be in place to address CSRF attacks and other security incidents promptly. These plans should include procedures for detecting and mitigating CSRF attacks, as well as communication strategies for informing affected users and stakeholders.

In summary, Cross-Site Request Forgery (CSRF) is a significant web application security vulnerability that can lead to unauthorized actions being performed on behalf of users. CSRF attacks exploit the trust that web applications place in users' browsers and can have serious consequences, including data loss and financial damage. Defending against CSRF attacks requires a combination of measures, including anti-CSRF tokens, same-site cookies, CORS policies, and user education. Developers, administrators, and security professionals should work together to implement these measures and regularly test their effectiveness to protect against CSRF attacks effectively.

Preventing Cross-Site Request Forgery (CSRF) attacks is crucial for the security of web applications and the protection of user data. CSRF attacks exploit the trust that web applications place in users' browsers, tricking them into performing actions without their consent. To effectively prevent CSRF attacks, web developers and organizations should implement robust security measures. One of the primary defenses against CSRF attacks is the use of anti-CSRF tokens. These tokens are unique and random values generated by the server and included in forms or requests. When a user submits a form or performs an action, the anti-CSRF token must be included and validated by the server to ensure the request is legitimate.

Anti-CSRF tokens act as a safeguard against CSRF attacks because an attacker would not have access to the token value. Even if an attacker tricks a user into making a request, they would not be able to include the correct anti-CSRF token, and the request would fail the server's validation.

Implementing same-site cookies is another effective measure to prevent CSRF attacks. Same-site cookies restrict the scope of cookies to the same site from which they originated. By setting the "SameSite" attribute on cookies, web applications can prevent browsers from sending authentication tokens to cross-site requests, making CSRF attacks less effective.

Cross-Origin Resource Sharing (CORS) policies are essential for controlling which domains are allowed to make cross-origin requests to a web application. By specifying these policies, web applications can restrict access to their resources and prevent unauthorized actions on behalf of users.

Session management practices play a crucial role in CSRF prevention. Web applications should ensure that session tokens are adequately protected and that users are authenticated before performing sensitive actions. Session tokens should have a short lifespan and be renewed regularly to minimize their exposure to potential attackers.

Avoiding predictable URLs for sensitive actions is another important aspect of CSRF prevention. Sensitive actions, such as changing a password or initiating a financial transaction, should not be accessible through easily guessable or predictable URLs. By using unpredictable and non-obvious URLs or endpoints, web applications can reduce the risk of CSRF attacks.

User education is an essential component of CSRF prevention. Users should be informed about the risks associated with clicking on suspicious links or visiting untrusted websites while logged into sensitive accounts. Understanding the potential consequences of CSRF attacks empowers users to take precautions to safeguard their accounts.

Regular web application security testing, including vulnerability scanning and penetration testing, is necessary to identify and address CSRF vulnerabilities.

Testing helps ensure that security measures are effective and that any potential weaknesses are discovered and remedied.

Incident response plans should be in place to address CSRF attacks and other security incidents promptly. These plans should include procedures for detecting and mitigating CSRF attacks, as well as communication strategies for informing affected users and stakeholders.

Developers should follow secure coding practices to minimize the risk of introducing CSRF vulnerabilities into their applications. These practices include validating input, encoding output, and implementing proper authentication and authorization controls.

Security frameworks and libraries that include built-in CSRF protection mechanisms can be valuable tools for developers. These tools often come with predefined secure settings and features that can enhance the overall security of web applications.

Regularly applying security patches and updates is essential for preventing CSRF attacks. Software vendors release patches to address known vulnerabilities, and failing to apply these updates leaves systems exposed to known exploits. Attackers actively search for unpatched systems to exploit.

In summary, preventing CSRF attacks is essential for maintaining the security of web applications and protecting user data. To effectively prevent CSRF attacks, web developers and organizations should implement anti-CSRF tokens, same-site cookies, CORS policies, and robust session management practices. User education, security testing, and incident response plans are also crucial elements of CSRF prevention. By following these measures and best practices, organizations can significantly reduce the risk of CSRF attacks and enhance the overall security posture of their web applications.

Chapter 9: Using Components with Known Vulnerabilities

Understanding the risks associated with vulnerable components is vital for maintaining the security of software applications and systems. Vulnerable components, such as libraries, frameworks, and third-party dependencies, are potential entry points for attackers looking to exploit known vulnerabilities. These components can introduce security weaknesses that may lead to data breaches, system compromise, and other adverse consequences.

One significant risk of vulnerable components is the exploitation of known vulnerabilities. Attackers often target well-known and widely used libraries or frameworks because they are more likely to discover vulnerabilities and exploit them. By exploiting known vulnerabilities, attackers can gain unauthorized access, manipulate data, or compromise the security of an application.

The risk of zero-day vulnerabilities is also associated with vulnerable components. Zero-day vulnerabilities are security weaknesses that are not publicly known or have not yet been patched by the software vendor. While less common than known vulnerabilities, zero-day vulnerabilities can have severe consequences if discovered and exploited by attackers.

Inadequate or irregular patching and updating of vulnerable components pose a significant risk. When software vendors release patches and updates to address known vulnerabilities, failing to apply these updates promptly leaves systems exposed to known exploits.

Attackers actively search for unpatched systems to exploit, making timely updates critical for security.

The risk of supply chain attacks is closely tied to vulnerable components. Attackers may compromise the software supply chain by inserting malicious code into widely used components during the development or distribution process. When organizations unknowingly use compromised components, they expose themselves to security risks.

Vulnerable components can also introduce risks related to compliance and regulatory requirements. Many industries have specific security standards and regulations that organizations must adhere to, such as the Payment Card Industry Data Security Standard (PCI DSS) or the Health Insurance Portability and Accountability Act (HIPAA). Using vulnerable components can result in non-compliance and legal consequences.

The risk of data breaches is significant when vulnerable components are exploited. Attackers can use vulnerabilities in components to gain access to sensitive data, including personally identifiable information (PII), financial records, or intellectual property. Data breaches can have severe financial, reputational, and legal implications for organizations.

Web application security risks are also associated with vulnerable components. Web applications often rely on libraries and frameworks for functionality. If these components have known vulnerabilities, attackers can exploit them to compromise the security of the web application, leading to defacement, data theft, or unauthorized access.

The risk of remote code execution is a concern with vulnerable components. Attackers may leverage vulnerabilities in components to execute arbitrary code on a target system. This can result in complete control of the system, allowing attackers to install malware, steal data, or launch further attacks.

The risk of denial-of-service (DoS) attacks is another consequence of vulnerable components. Attackers can exploit vulnerabilities to overwhelm a system or application with traffic, causing it to become unresponsive or crash. DoS attacks can disrupt operations and lead to service outages.

Reputation damage is a significant risk when vulnerable components are exploited. Customers and stakeholders expect organizations to prioritize security and protect their data. A security incident resulting from vulnerable components can erode trust and tarnish an organization's reputation.

The risk of financial losses is associated with vulnerable components due to the costs of addressing security incidents, regulatory fines, legal fees, and potential revenue loss. Organizations may incur substantial financial burdens when responding to security breaches caused by vulnerable components.

Mitigating the risks associated with vulnerable components requires a proactive approach to software security. Organizations should implement the following strategies and best practices:

Regularly monitor and assess third-party components for known vulnerabilities. Use automated tools and services that can identify vulnerabilities in libraries and frameworks used in your software.

Establish a patch management process that ensures timely updates and patches for vulnerable components. Keep an inventory of all components used and regularly check for updates or security advisories.

Prioritize critical and high-risk vulnerabilities for immediate remediation. Not all vulnerabilities have the same impact, so focus on addressing the most severe ones first.

Conduct thorough security testing, including vulnerability scanning and penetration testing, to identify and address vulnerabilities in your software.

Implement security controls and mechanisms, such as web application firewalls (WAFs), intrusion detection systems (IDS), and security information and event management (SIEM) solutions, to detect and respond to security incidents related to vulnerable components.

Educate developers and IT teams about the risks associated with vulnerable components and best practices for secure software development.

Establish a secure software development lifecycle (SDLC) that includes security assessments and reviews of third-party components before their integration into software projects.

Monitor and stay informed about security news and advisories related to third-party components. Subscribe to security mailing lists and notifications from software vendors and organizations that track vulnerabilities.

Consider using software composition analysis (SCA) tools to automatically identify and manage vulnerable components in your software supply chain.

Maintain an incident response plan that outlines procedures for addressing security incidents related to vulnerable components. This plan should include communication strategies for informing affected users and stakeholders.

In summary, the risks associated with vulnerable components are a significant concern for organizations and their software applications. These risks include the exploitation of known vulnerabilities, the potential for zero-day vulnerabilities, supply chain attacks, compliance and regulatory issues, data breaches, web application security risks, and more. Mitigating these risks requires a proactive and comprehensive approach to software security, including regular monitoring, patch management, security testing, education, and incident response planning. By following best practices and staying vigilant, organizations can reduce their exposure to the risks associated with vulnerable components and enhance the overall security of their software systems.

Effectively managing component vulnerabilities is a critical aspect of maintaining the security and integrity of software applications and systems. Vulnerable components, such as libraries, frameworks, and third-party dependencies, can introduce security weaknesses that attackers may exploit. To address this challenge, organizations need to implement robust strategies for identifying, assessing, and mitigating component vulnerabilities.

One key strategy for managing component vulnerabilities is to maintain an up-to-date inventory of all components used in an organization's software projects. This inventory should include details such as version numbers, licensing information, and the source of each component. Having a comprehensive inventory allows organizations to quickly identify and track vulnerabilities in their software supply chain.

Regularly monitoring for security advisories and updates related to components is essential. Organizations should subscribe to mailing lists and notifications from software vendors, security organizations, and open-source projects that track and report vulnerabilities. Staying informed about the latest security advisories helps organizations take timely action to address vulnerabilities.

Prioritizing vulnerabilities based on severity and impact is a crucial step in managing component vulnerabilities. Not all vulnerabilities are created equal, and organizations should focus their efforts on addressing high-risk vulnerabilities that pose the most significant threats. Prioritization allows organizations to allocate resources effectively and address the most critical issues first.

Implementing an effective patch management process is essential for addressing component vulnerabilities promptly. Organizations should establish procedures for applying security patches and updates as soon as they become available. This process should include testing patches in a controlled environment before deploying them in production.

Performing regular security assessments, including vulnerability scanning and penetration testing, is another key strategy for managing component vulnerabilities. Security assessments help identify vulnerabilities in both the organization's code and third-party components. Regular testing provides insights into the security posture of software applications and systems.

Educating developers and IT teams about the risks associated with component vulnerabilities and best practices for secure development is crucial. Awareness and training programs can help organizations build a culture of security and ensure that teams are proactive in addressing vulnerabilities.

Integrating security into the software development lifecycle (SDLC) is essential for managing component vulnerabilities effectively. This includes conducting security assessments and reviews of third-party components before their integration into software projects. By identifying and addressing vulnerabilities early in the development process, organizations can reduce the likelihood of security issues making their way into production.

Implementing security controls and mechanisms, such as web application firewalls (WAFs), intrusion detection systems (IDS), and security information and event management (SIEM) solutions, can help detect and respond to security incidents related to component vulnerabilities. These controls add an additional layer of defense and enhance the organization's ability to monitor and protect against threats.

Engaging in responsible disclosure practices is important when organizations discover vulnerabilities in third-party components. Organizations should report vulnerabilities to the component's maintainers or the appropriate security coordination center and work collaboratively to address the issue. Responsible disclosure helps ensure that vulnerabilities are patched promptly and does not expose users to unnecessary risks.

Creating an incident response plan that outlines procedures for addressing security incidents related to component vulnerabilities is essential. This plan should include communication strategies for informing affected users and stakeholders and should be tested regularly to ensure its effectiveness.

Implementing software composition analysis (SCA) tools can automate the process of identifying and managing component vulnerabilities in an organization's software supply chain. SCA tools can scan software projects for known vulnerabilities in third-party components, provide information on available patches and updates, and assist in prioritizing remediation efforts.

Performing risk assessments to evaluate the potential impact of component vulnerabilities on the organization is a proactive strategy. Risk assessments help organizations understand the business and operational risks associated with specific vulnerabilities, allowing them to make informed decisions about prioritization and resource allocation.

Collaborating with the broader security community, including sharing threat intelligence and best practices, can enhance an organization's ability to manage component vulnerabilities effectively. Participating in information-sharing initiatives and industry-specific security groups helps organizations stay informed about emerging threats and mitigation strategies.

Monitoring the security of the software supply chain is an ongoing effort. Organizations should continuously evaluate the security posture of their components, assess new vulnerabilities as they emerge, and update their mitigation strategies accordingly.

In summary, managing component vulnerabilities is a critical aspect of software security. Organizations should maintain component inventories, monitor for security advisories, prioritize vulnerabilities, implement patch management processes, conduct security assessments, educate teams, integrate security into the SDLC, and use security controls. Responsible disclosure, incident response planning, and risk assessments are also important strategies. Automation through SCA tools and collaboration with the security community further strengthen an organization's ability to manage component vulnerabilities effectively. By adopting these strategies, organizations can reduce the risks associated with component vulnerabilities and enhance the overall security of their software applications and systems.

Chapter 10: Unvalidated Redirects and Forwards: The Art of Deception

Unvalidated redirects and forwards are security vulnerabilities that can pose a significant risk to web applications. These vulnerabilities occur when web applications allow user-supplied input to control the destination of redirects or forwards without proper validation. In essence, unvalidated redirects and forwards can enable attackers to redirect users to malicious websites or perform unauthorized actions.

The core issue with unvalidated redirects and forwards lies in the lack of validation and trust in user input. Web applications often use redirects and forwards to enhance user experience by redirecting users to different pages or websites, but if the destination is controlled by user input, it can become a security risk.

Attackers can exploit unvalidated redirects and forwards to conduct phishing attacks, steal sensitive information, or perform actions on behalf of unsuspecting users. For example, if a web application has a feature that allows users to be redirected to external websites, an attacker can craft a malicious link that appears legitimate but actually redirects the user to a malicious site.

The impact of unvalidated redirects and forwards can vary depending on the specific use case and functionality of the web application. In some cases, it may lead to users being tricked into disclosing sensitive information, such as login credentials or financial data, to malicious actors.

To mitigate the risk of unvalidated redirects and forwards, web applications should implement proper validation and security controls. Here are some key strategies and best practices:

Validate and Sanitize User Input: Ensure that any user-supplied input used to control redirects or forwards is thoroughly validated and sanitized. This includes checking the input for validity, ensuring it does not contain malicious code, and restricting it to only allowed values or patterns.

Use Whitelists: Maintain a whitelist of trusted destinations or URLs to which redirects and forwards are allowed. Ensure that any destination not on the whitelist is rejected.

Avoid User-Controlled Destinations: Whenever possible, avoid allowing users to control the destination of redirects or forwards. If user-controlled redirects are necessary, use additional security measures, such as tokens or session checks, to ensure that users can only redirect to authorized destinations.

Implement Safe Redirect Mechanisms: Use safe and predictable redirection mechanisms provided by the programming language or framework used. Avoid using mechanisms that rely solely on user input to determine the destination.

Educate Users: Educate users about the risks of following external links and provide guidance on verifying the authenticity of URLs before clicking on them.

Regularly Test for Vulnerabilities: Conduct regular security testing, including vulnerability scanning and penetration testing, to identify and address unvalidated redirects and forwards in your web application.

Leverage Security Libraries and Tools: Consider using security libraries and tools that provide protection against unvalidated redirects and forwards. These tools often come with built-in security features that can help prevent such vulnerabilities.

Implement Proper Access Controls: Ensure that users are authorized to access the destination to which they are being redirected. Implement access controls and authentication checks as needed.

Logging and Monitoring: Implement logging and monitoring to detect and respond to suspicious redirection activities. Monitor for unusual patterns or excessive redirects that could indicate an attack.

Incident Response: Develop an incident response plan that includes procedures for responding to incidents related to unvalidated redirects and forwards. This plan should include communication strategies for informing affected users and stakeholders.

In summary, unvalidated redirects and forwards are security vulnerabilities that can have serious implications for web applications and their users. These vulnerabilities occur when web applications allow user input to control redirection destinations without proper validation. Attackers can exploit these vulnerabilities for phishing attacks and to trick users into visiting malicious websites. To mitigate the risks associated with unvalidated redirects and forwards, web applications should implement robust validation, use whitelists, avoid user-controlled destinations, and educate users about the risks. Regular testing, security tools, proper access controls, and incident response planning are also essential elements of a comprehensive security strategy to protect against these vulnerabilities.

Preventing deceptive redirects and forwards is crucial for maintaining the security and trustworthiness of web applications. Deceptive redirects and forwards occur when attackers manipulate the destination of redirects or forwards to trick users into visiting malicious websites or disclosing sensitive information. To counter this threat, web developers and organizations need to implement effective techniques to protect against deceptive redirection.

One of the primary techniques for preventing deceptive redirects and forwards is to validate and sanitize all user input used to control redirection destinations. This validation process should include checking the input for correctness, ensuring it does not contain malicious code or unexpected characters, and verifying that it adheres to predefined patterns or formats.

Using whitelists is another effective technique to thwart deceptive redirects and forwards. By maintaining a whitelist of trusted destinations or URLs to which redirects and forwards are permitted, organizations can restrict user input to only those destinations that are known and verified to be safe.

Avoiding user-controlled destinations whenever possible is a recommended best practice. When users have control over where a redirect or forward leads, it opens the door to potential abuse. If user-controlled redirects are necessary, consider implementing additional security measures, such as tokens or session checks, to ensure that users can only redirect to authorized destinations.

Implementing safe and predictable redirection mechanisms provided by the programming language or framework used is essential. These mechanisms often have built-in security features that help protect against deceptive redirects and forwards. Avoid using mechanisms that rely solely on user input to determine the destination, as they can be easily manipulated.

Educating users about the risks of following external links and providing guidance on how to verify the authenticity of URLs before clicking on them is an essential preventive technique. Informed users are less likely to fall victim to deceptive redirects and forwards.

Regular security testing is a critical technique to identify and address vulnerabilities related to deceptive redirects and forwards. Conducting vulnerability scanning and penetration testing helps organizations discover and remediate security weaknesses in their web applications, including those that may lead to deceptive redirection.

Leveraging security libraries and tools designed to protect against deceptive redirects and forwards is highly advisable. These tools often come with built-in security features that can help prevent such vulnerabilities and enhance the overall security of web applications.

Proper access controls are essential for preventing unauthorized redirection. Organizations should ensure that users are authorized to access the destination to which they are being redirected. Implement access controls and authentication checks as needed to prevent misuse.

Logging and monitoring are crucial for detecting and responding to suspicious redirection activities. By implementing robust logging and monitoring mechanisms, organizations can identify unusual patterns or excessive redirects that may indicate an attack. Timely detection can lead to quicker mitigation efforts.

Developing an incident response plan that outlines procedures for responding to incidents related to deceptive redirects and forwards is essential. This plan should include communication strategies for informing affected users and stakeholders, as well as clear steps for addressing and resolving security incidents.

Incorporating the use of software composition analysis (SCA) tools is a practical way to automate the identification and management of deceptive redirects and forwards in an organization's software supply chain. SCA tools can scan software projects for known vulnerabilities in third-party components, provide information on available patches and updates, and assist in prioritizing remediation efforts.

Risk assessments can help organizations evaluate the potential impact of deceptive redirects and forwards on their operations and reputation. By conducting risk assessments, organizations can better understand the business and operational risks associated with specific vulnerabilities and make informed decisions about mitigation.

Collaboration with the broader security community and sharing threat intelligence and best practices can enhance an organization's ability to prevent deceptive redirects and forwards effectively. Participating in information-sharing initiatives and industry-specific security groups provides valuable insights into emerging threats and mitigation strategies.

In summary, deceptive redirects and forwards are serious security risks that can undermine the trustworthiness of web applications and expose users to harm. These vulnerabilities occur when attackers manipulate redirection destinations to deceive users into visiting malicious websites or disclosing sensitive information. To prevent deceptive redirection, web developers and organizations should implement techniques such as input validation, whitelists, safe redirection mechanisms, user education, security testing, security tools, access controls, logging, and incident response planning. Automated tools like SCA can also assist in identifying and managing vulnerabilities. Risk assessments and collaboration with the security community further strengthen an organization's ability to protect against deceptive redirects and forwards and enhance the overall security of their web applications.

BOOK 2
MASTERING OWASP TOP 10
A COMPREHENSIVE GUIDE TO WEB APPLICATION
SECURITY

ROB BOTWRIGHT

Chapter 1: Deep Dive into the OWASP Top 10

The OWASP Top 10 is a widely recognized and influential document in the field of web application security. It serves as a guide to the most critical web application security risks. The OWASP Top 10 provides a valuable resource for developers, security professionals, and organizations to understand and prioritize security issues. It offers insight into the vulnerabilities and threats that are most likely to impact web applications. By highlighting the top security risks, the OWASP Top 10 helps organizations allocate resources and focus on the areas that pose the greatest danger. Web application security is a critical concern in today's digital landscape, with an ever-increasing number of applications being developed and deployed. The significance of the OWASP Top 10 lies in its ability to raise awareness about the most common and potentially devastating security vulnerabilities. It provides a common language for discussing security issues and enables organizations to make informed decisions about their security posture. The OWASP Top 10 is not a static document; it is regularly updated to reflect the evolving threat landscape. This ensures that it remains relevant and applicable to the latest security challenges. The Top 10 list is based on data and input from security experts, making it a credible and trusted resource. One of the key benefits of the OWASP Top 10 is its role in driving improvements in web application security practices. It encourages developers and organizations to take proactive steps to mitigate security risks. The Top 10 list is a valuable tool for training and educating developers about secure coding practices. It provides practical examples and guidance on how to avoid common pitfalls. By following the recommendations in the OWASP Top 10, developers can write more secure code and reduce the likelihood of vulnerabilities. The document is not only beneficial for developers but also for security professionals responsible for assessing and testing web applications. It helps them prioritize their efforts and focus on the vulnerabilities that are most likely to be exploited by attackers. The OWASP Top 10 can also serve as a benchmark for organizations to measure their security posture. They can use it as a reference point to assess their applications and determine where improvements are needed. The Top 10 list helps organizations understand the consequences of security vulnerabilities in terms of data breaches, financial losses, and reputational damage. It underscores the importance of proactive security measures to prevent costly incidents. Another significant aspect of the OWASP Top 10 is its role in compliance and regulatory requirements. Many industry-specific regulations, such as the Payment Card Industry Data Security Standard (PCI DSS) and the Health Insurance Portability and Accountability Act (HIPAA), reference the Top 10 as a security standard. Organizations that handle sensitive data must adhere to these regulations, making the OWASP Top 10 a critical reference. The OWASP Top 10 also promotes the adoption of secure development practices throughout the software development lifecycle. It encourages organizations to integrate security into their processes from the early stages of application design and development. By considering security from the outset, organizations can reduce the cost and effort required to address vulnerabilities later in the development cycle. The Top 10 list is a valuable resource for raising awareness about the importance of web application security among stakeholders, including executives, managers, and board members. It helps them understand the business risks associated with security vulnerabilities and the need for investment in security measures. The OWASP Top 10 provides a common framework for communication between security teams and development teams. It fosters collaboration and ensures that security concerns are adequately addressed throughout the development process. The document is a practical guide for organizations seeking to improve their security posture without the need for in-depth technical expertise. It offers actionable recommendations that can be implemented by organizations of all sizes. The OWASP Top 10 serves as a foundation for more advanced security practices and frameworks. It provides a starting point for organizations looking to build a robust and comprehensive security program. The Top 10 list helps organizations prioritize their security investments and allocate resources efficiently. It enables them to focus on the vulnerabilities and threats that have the greatest potential impact on their applications and business. The OWASP Top 10 is a living document that evolves to keep pace with emerging threats and changing technologies. It adapts to new attack vectors and vulnerabilities, making it a dynamic and relevant resource. The document is not limited to a specific technology or programming language. It applies to a wide range of web applications, making it applicable to diverse development environments. The OWASP Top 10 is a valuable resource for security professionals and organizations seeking to stay ahead of evolving threats. It provides a roadmap for improving web application security and reducing the risk of security breaches. The Top 10 list has a global reach, with organizations and security experts around the world referencing and using it as a foundation for their security efforts. In summary, the significance of the OWASP Top 10 lies in its role as a comprehensive and widely accepted guide to web application security. It offers practical advice, promotes secure development practices, and helps organizations prioritize their security efforts. By addressing the vulnerabilities and threats outlined in the Top 10 list, organizations can enhance the security of their web applications and protect against potential risks. Interpreting OWASP Top 10 data is crucial for understanding the current state of web application security. Data from the OWASP Top 10 can provide valuable insights into the prevalence and severity of common security vulnerabilities. Interpretation of this data requires careful analysis and consideration of various factors. One of the first steps in interpreting OWASP Top 10 data is to review the specific vulnerabilities listed in the report. Each vulnerability is accompanied by a description and details about its impact and potential exploitation. Understanding the nature of these vulnerabilities is essential for assessing their significance. The next step is to analyze the data on the frequency of each vulnerability. This data typically includes statistics on how often each vulnerability has been identified in real-world applications. High-frequency vulnerabilities may indicate widespread security issues that require immediate attention. Severity ratings associated with each vulnerability are another critical aspect of the data. These ratings provide insights into the potential impact of exploitation. Vulnerabilities with higher severity ratings may pose more significant risks to organizations. Examining the historical trends in OWASP Top 10 data is essential. Comparing data from previous years can reveal whether the prevalence of certain vulnerabilities is increasing or decreasing. Trends can also shed light on emerging security challenges. It's important to consider the industries and sectors that are most affected by the vulnerabilities listed in the OWASP Top 10. Some vulnerabilities may be more prevalent in specific industries, making it necessary to tailor security strategies accordingly. Geographical data can also be valuable when interpreting OWASP Top 10 data. Analyzing where certain vulnerabilities are more common can help organizations focus their security efforts on high-risk regions. Understanding the root causes of vulnerabilities is critical. Some vulnerabilities may result from coding errors, while others may be related to misconfigurations or design flaws. Identifying the root causes can guide organizations in implementing effective remediation strategies. Organizations should also examine the consequences of exploiting OWASP Top 10 vulnerabilities. This can include data breaches, financial losses, and reputational damage. Understanding the potential impact of these vulnerabilities can drive home the importance of addressing them. Interpreting OWASP Top 10 data requires consideration of the impact on different stakeholders. Developers, security teams, executives, and customers all have a vested interest in the security of web applications. Tailoring the interpretation to address the concerns and priorities of each stakeholder group is essential. Organizations should also analyze the data in the context of their specific applications and technologies. Some vulnerabilities may be more relevant to certain types of applications or programming languages. Customizing the interpretation ensures that organizations address vulnerabilities that are most pertinent to their environment. Benchmarking data against industry standards and best practices can provide valuable context. Comparing OWASP Top 10 data to established security benchmarks can help organizations gauge their security posture relative to peers and industry norms. Interpreting data from real-world incidents and breaches can provide additional context. Studying how vulnerabilities have been exploited in actual attacks can shed light on the tactics and techniques used by attackers. This knowledge can inform defense strategies. Consideration of the time and resources required to address OWASP Top 10 vulnerabilities is vital. Organizations must balance the urgency of remediation with the available resources and timelines. Prioritizing vulnerabilities based on their potential impact and the feasibility of remediation is a key aspect of interpretation. Interpreting OWASP Top 10 data is an ongoing process. Organizations should regularly review and update their interpretation to reflect changing circumstances and emerging threats. Engaging with the broader security community and sharing insights can enhance the interpretation of OWASP Top 10 data. Collaboration with experts and peers can lead to more informed and effective security strategies. In summary, interpreting OWASP Top 10 data is a critical component of web application security. It involves analyzing the nature, frequency, severity, and trends of vulnerabilities. Understanding the root causes and consequences of these vulnerabilities is essential. Interpretation should consider the impact on various stakeholders, the specific context of an organization, and relevant industry standards. It should also factor in resource constraints and prioritize remediation efforts. Regularly updating and refining the interpretation process ensures that organizations stay resilient against evolving threats.

Chapter 2: Exploring Injection Attacks and Mitigations

Understanding injection attacks is crucial for safeguarding web applications against a common and severe security threat. Injection attacks are a class of vulnerabilities where an attacker can manipulate data inputs to execute malicious commands or queries. These attacks can target various types of data, including SQL queries, code, and even operating system commands. The most well-known type of injection attack is SQL injection, where an attacker inserts malicious SQL code into user inputs. The goal of injection attacks is to manipulate an application's logic to perform actions that were not intended by the developers. The consequences of successful injection attacks can be severe, ranging from data breaches to unauthorized system access.

Injection attacks often target web applications that interact with databases or external systems. Attackers exploit vulnerabilities in the way user inputs are handled and processed by the application. The term "injection" derives from the attacker injecting malicious code or data into the application's input fields or parameters. SQL injection, for example, occurs when an attacker inserts SQL code into a web application's input fields. This malicious SQL code can then be executed by the application's database, potentially revealing, modifying, or deleting sensitive data.

Another common type of injection attack is command injection, which targets the execution of operating system commands. Attackers input malicious commands into an application's input fields, and if not properly sanitized or validated, these commands are executed by the underlying system. Command injection can lead to system compromise and unauthorized access to sensitive resources.

Cross-site Scripting (XSS) attacks, while not strictly injection attacks, also involve injecting malicious code into web applications. In XSS attacks, the injected code is typically executed within the context of a user's web browser, allowing attackers to steal session cookies, deface websites, or redirect users to malicious sites.

To understand injection attacks better, it's essential to explore their characteristics and how they can be prevented.

Injection attacks take advantage of vulnerabilities in input validation and sanitization. Developers often assume that users will provide legitimate input, but attackers exploit this trust to insert malicious code. The root cause of injection attacks is the failure to distinguish between data and code within user inputs.

SQL injection, for instance, occurs when user inputs are directly concatenated into SQL queries without proper validation. In such cases, attackers can manipulate the input to modify the query's logic, potentially accessing unauthorized data.

Command injection attacks similarly occur when user inputs are used to construct system commands. Without adequate input validation, attackers can inject arbitrary commands, leading to unauthorized system operations.

The impact of injection attacks can be far-reaching. Successful attacks can result in data breaches, where sensitive information is exposed or stolen. In the case of

SQL injection, attackers can extract data from databases, including usernames, passwords, and confidential records. In command injection attacks, unauthorized system commands can be executed, potentially compromising the entire system. Such attacks may lead to data loss, service disruption, and even complete system compromise.

To prevent injection attacks, developers and organizations must adopt secure coding practices. Input validation and sanitization are fundamental defenses against injection vulnerabilities. Developers should validate and sanitize all user inputs before using them in queries, commands, or other critical operations.

Parameterized queries and prepared statements are effective techniques for preventing SQL injection. By separating user inputs from query logic, these methods ensure that malicious SQL code cannot be injected.

Similarly, using safe and validated inputs for system commands can prevent command injection attacks. Avoiding the use of user inputs to construct commands and employing proper input validation is crucial.

Web application firewalls (WAFs) can provide an additional layer of protection against injection attacks. WAFs analyze incoming traffic and can block requests that exhibit suspicious behavior indicative of injection attempts.

Regular security testing, including vulnerability scanning and penetration testing, can help identify and remediate injection vulnerabilities. Testing can uncover weaknesses in input validation and provide insights into potential attack vectors.

Educating developers and security teams about injection attacks is essential. Awareness and training programs can help them understand the risks and adopt secure coding practices.

Security by design is a holistic approach that incorporates security considerations into every phase of the software development lifecycle. By prioritizing security from the outset, organizations can minimize the risk of injection vulnerabilities.

Monitoring and logging are crucial for detecting and responding to injection attacks in real-time. Monitoring can help identify suspicious activity, while logging can provide a record of incidents for further analysis.

In summary, understanding injection attacks is vital for securing web applications against these prevalent threats. Injection attacks target vulnerabilities in input validation and can have severe consequences, including data breaches and system compromise. Preventing injection attacks requires secure coding practices, input validation, parameterized queries, and proper command handling. Security testing, education, and monitoring play essential roles in defending against injection vulnerabilities. By adopting these measures, organizations can mitigate the risk of injection attacks and enhance the security of their web applications.

Effective mitigation strategies for injection vulnerabilities are essential for securing web applications against these common and potentially devastating attacks. Injection vulnerabilities, including SQL injection and command injection, occur when attackers manipulate user inputs to execute malicious code or queries. Mitigating these vulnerabilities requires a multi-faceted approach that encompasses both proactive and reactive measures. A fundamental strategy for mitigating injection vulnerabilities is to implement input validation and sanitization. Developers should rigorously validate and sanitize all user inputs to ensure that they contain only safe and expected data. This process involves checking input for valid data types, length, and format, and rejecting any inputs that do not meet these criteria.

Parameterized queries and prepared statements are powerful tools for preventing SQL injection attacks. These techniques allow developers to separate user inputs from SQL query logic, ensuring that user inputs are treated as data rather than executable code. By using parameterized queries, developers can significantly reduce the risk of SQL injection vulnerabilities.

Similarly, for command injection vulnerabilities, it's crucial to avoid constructing system commands from user inputs. Developers should design their applications to use safe and trusted inputs for any commands that interact with the underlying operating system. Input validation should be applied rigorously to any user-provided data used in command construction.

Web application firewalls (WAFs) are an additional layer of defense against injection attacks. WAFs analyze incoming traffic and can block requests that exhibit suspicious patterns or characteristics indicative of injection attempts. While WAFs are not a panacea, they can provide valuable protection against known injection attacks and emerging threats.

Security testing, including vulnerability scanning and penetration testing, is an essential part of mitigating injection vulnerabilities. Regularly testing web applications can help identify and address weaknesses in input validation and other security controls. Testing should be an ongoing process to ensure that vulnerabilities are continuously monitored and remediated.

Educating developers and security teams about injection vulnerabilities and secure coding practices is crucial. Awareness and training programs can help individuals understand the risks and challenges associated with injection attacks. By fostering a security-conscious culture, organizations can reduce the likelihood of injection vulnerabilities making their way into production code.

Security by design is a holistic approach that incorporates security considerations into every phase of the software development lifecycle. By prioritizing security from the outset, organizations can minimize the risk of injection vulnerabilities. Security reviews and threat modeling exercises can help identify potential injection points and design secure solutions.

Implementing monitoring and logging is essential for detecting and responding to injection attacks in real-time. Monitoring can help identify unusual or suspicious activity that may indicate an ongoing attack. Logging provides a valuable record of incidents for forensic analysis and incident response.

Incident response planning is a critical aspect of mitigating injection vulnerabilities. Organizations should develop and maintain incident response plans that outline procedures for detecting, containing, and mitigating injection attacks. These plans should also include communication strategies for informing affected users and stakeholders.

Regularly patching and updating software components is crucial for mitigating injection vulnerabilities. Many injection attacks target known vulnerabilities in software libraries and frameworks. By keeping software up to date, organizations can reduce their exposure to these types of attacks.

Leveraging security libraries and tools designed to prevent injection attacks can enhance an organization's security posture. These tools often come with built-in security features that can help protect against injection vulnerabilities. Using security libraries can simplify the process of implementing secure coding practices.

Strategic access controls and least privilege principles are essential for mitigating injection vulnerabilities. By ensuring that users and processes have only the necessary access rights and permissions, organizations can limit the potential impact of successful injection attacks.

Security headers, such as Content Security Policy (CSP) and Cross-Origin Resource Sharing (CORS) policies, can provide additional protection against injection attacks. These headers define how web browsers should handle content and resources, helping to mitigate the risk of certain types of attacks, including XSS attacks.

Network-level controls, such as firewalls and intrusion detection systems (IDS), can also contribute to the mitigation of injection vulnerabilities. Firewalls can filter incoming traffic to block malicious requests, while IDS can detect and alert on suspicious behavior indicative of injection attempts.

Effective documentation and knowledge sharing within an organization can ensure that developers and security teams are aware of best practices for mitigating injection vulnerabilities. Maintaining up-to-date documentation and sharing knowledge about security controls and mitigations can help prevent injection vulnerabilities from recurring.

In summary, effective mitigation strategies for injection vulnerabilities are essential for safeguarding web applications against these pervasive threats. Mitigation efforts should encompass input validation, parameterized queries, security testing, education, monitoring, incident response planning, patch management, security tools, access controls, security headers, and network-level controls. A comprehensive approach that combines proactive measures with reactive responses can significantly reduce the risk of injection vulnerabilities and enhance the security of web applications.

Chapter 3: Strengthening Authentication and Session Management

Implementing secure authentication practices is fundamental for protecting user accounts and sensitive data in web applications. Authentication is the process of verifying the identity of users attempting to access a system or application. Weak or insecure authentication mechanisms can lead to unauthorized access, data breaches, and compromised user accounts. To ensure secure authentication, developers and organizations should follow best practices that strengthen the authentication process.

One of the core principles of secure authentication is the use of strong and unique passwords. Passwords are a common form of authentication, and they should be complex, lengthy, and difficult for attackers to guess. Encouraging users to create strong passwords and enforcing password complexity rules can help prevent brute-force and dictionary attacks.

Implementing multi-factor authentication (MFA) is a highly effective way to enhance security. MFA requires users to provide multiple forms of identification before granting access. This typically involves something the user knows (e.g., a password) and something the user has (e.g., a mobile device with an authentication app). MFA significantly reduces the risk of unauthorized access, even if an attacker obtains a user's password.

Avoid storing passwords in plaintext or using weak hashing algorithms. Passwords should be securely hashed and salted before storage. Salting involves adding a random value to each user's password before hashing it, making it more challenging for attackers to use precomputed rainbow tables for password cracking.

Implement account lockout policies to thwart brute-force attacks. Account lockout policies can temporarily or permanently lock out users who repeatedly enter incorrect credentials. However, organizations should strike a balance between security and usability, as overly aggressive lockout policies can lead to user frustration.

Implement strong session management practices. Sessions should have a finite lifespan and automatically log users out after a period of inactivity. Additionally, ensure that session tokens are securely generated and managed to prevent session fixation attacks.

Use secure communication protocols, such as HTTPS, to protect login credentials during transmission. Unencrypted communication can expose login information to eavesdroppers. HTTPS encrypts data between the user's device and the server, providing a secure channel for authentication.

Implement proper account recovery and password reset procedures. These processes should include additional verification steps, such as sending a code to the user's email or mobile device. Account recovery should not rely solely on knowledge-based questions that an attacker could guess or discover.

Consider implementing adaptive authentication, which adjusts the authentication requirements based on risk factors. For example, high-risk login attempts from unfamiliar locations may trigger additional authentication steps. Adaptive authentication helps balance security and usability.

Regularly audit and monitor authentication logs for suspicious activities. Unusual login patterns, multiple failed login attempts, and unfamiliar devices should trigger alerts for further investigation. Continuous monitoring can help detect and respond to authentication-related threats promptly.

Educate users about secure authentication practices. Provide guidance on creating strong passwords, enabling MFA, and recognizing phishing attempts. Well-informed users are more likely to take steps to protect their accounts.

Implement secure password recovery mechanisms. Avoid sending passwords via email or other insecure channels. Instead, send temporary, time-limited links for password reset or account recovery.

Implement strong CAPTCHA or reCAPTCHA challenges to prevent automated attacks, such as brute-force or credential stuffing attacks. CAPTCHAs require users to solve puzzles or prove they are not bots, adding an extra layer of defense.

Securely store and manage user authentication data. Use industry-standard encryption and security practices to protect sensitive user information. Consider outsourcing authentication to trusted identity providers to reduce the risk associated with handling authentication data.

Implement secure single sign-on (SSO) solutions for users to access multiple applications with a single set of credentials. SSO reduces the need for users to remember multiple passwords and simplifies authentication management.

Regularly test and audit your authentication mechanisms for vulnerabilities. Penetration testing and security assessments can help identify weaknesses in the authentication process that attackers could exploit.

Implement strong security headers, such as HTTP Strict Transport Security (HSTS) and Content Security Policy (CSP), to protect against various web-based attacks, including session hijacking and cross-site scripting (XSS).

Regularly update and patch authentication components and libraries to address known vulnerabilities. Security updates help mitigate emerging threats and protect against newly discovered vulnerabilities.

Securely handle and protect authentication tokens. Tokens should not be exposed in URLs or stored in insecure locations, such as browser cookies. Implement measures to prevent token theft and misuse.

Consider implementing time-based one-time passwords (TOTP) or hardware tokens for MFA. These methods provide an additional layer of security by generating temporary codes that change periodically.

Educate your development and security teams about the latest authentication best practices and emerging threats. Staying informed and up-to-date is crucial in the rapidly evolving landscape of web application security.

In summary, secure authentication practices are essential for protecting user accounts and data in web applications. Implementing strong passwords, multi-factor authentication, secure communication, proper session management, and secure password recovery mechanisms are vital steps. Continuous monitoring, user education, and security testing are crucial for maintaining a robust authentication process. By following these best practices, organizations can enhance their security posture and reduce the risk of unauthorized access and data breaches.

Advanced session management techniques play a pivotal role in securing web applications and protecting user data from unauthorized access and misuse. Sessions are a fundamental component of web applications, enabling users to maintain their state and interact with the application seamlessly. However, without proper management and security measures, sessions can become vulnerable to attacks, compromising the confidentiality and integrity of user data. This chapter explores advanced techniques and strategies for enhancing session management in web applications.

Session fixation attacks are a significant concern in session management. In a session fixation attack, an attacker sets a user's session identifier, potentially gaining unauthorized access to the user's account. To defend against session fixation attacks, web applications can implement session regeneration techniques. When a user logs in or changes their authentication status, the application generates a new session identifier, rendering any existing session identifier invalid. This approach helps mitigate the risk of an attacker fixing a session identifier before a legitimate user logs in.

Session hijacking, also known as session theft or session sidejacking, is another common threat. In session hijacking attacks, attackers intercept or steal session identifiers, enabling them to impersonate legitimate users. To thwart session hijacking, web applications can adopt secure communication protocols, such as HTTPS. HTTPS encrypts data transmitted between the user's device and the server, preventing eavesdroppers from capturing session identifiers.

Implementing session timeout mechanisms is essential to mitigate session-related risks. Session timeouts automatically terminate idle sessions, reducing the window of opportunity for attackers to exploit them. Web applications can define session timeout periods based on user activity and sensitivity of data. For example, sensitive operations may have shorter session timeouts than less critical activities.

Cross-site scripting (XSS) attacks pose a threat to session management. In XSS attacks, malicious scripts injected into web pages can steal session identifiers or manipulate session data. To prevent XSS attacks, web applications can implement proper input validation and output encoding. Input validation ensures that user-provided data is sanitized and free of malicious scripts. Output encoding ensures that data displayed in web pages is treated as text, preventing script execution.

Secure cookies are a vital component of advanced session management. Cookies are used to store session identifiers and other session-related data on the user's device. Web applications can set secure and HttpOnly flags on cookies. The secure flag instructs the browser to send cookies only over HTTPS connections, reducing the risk of interception. The HttpOnly flag prevents JavaScript from accessing cookies, protecting session identifiers from client-side attacks.

Implementing role-based access controls (RBAC) within sessions enhances security. RBAC restricts users' access to specific resources and features based on their roles and privileges. By incorporating RBAC into session management, web applications can ensure that users can only perform actions aligned with their authorized roles.

Implementing session logging and monitoring provides insight into session activities. Logs can capture session creation, termination, and unusual behaviors, helping security teams identify suspicious activities. Monitoring tools can detect anomalies and alert administrators to potential session-related threats, allowing for timely responses.

To protect against session fixation attacks, web applications can implement session token rotation. This technique involves periodically changing session tokens, making it challenging for attackers to predict or fixate on token values. Session token rotation is particularly useful for long-lived sessions.

Implementing session revocation mechanisms is essential for dealing with compromised sessions. If a user reports a session compromise or if suspicious activities are detected, web applications should offer a mechanism to revoke the affected session. Session revocation ensures that even if an attacker gains access to a session identifier, they cannot continue to use it.

Implementing session persistence across server clusters requires advanced techniques. In distributed environments, where web applications run on multiple servers, session data must be synchronized and maintained consistently. Using techniques such as database-backed session storage or distributed caching systems can ensure that sessions remain intact and accessible across server clusters.

Implementing session encryption can enhance the security of sensitive session data. While session identifiers should be stored securely, some session data may still need additional protection. Encrypting session data, such as user credentials or sensitive settings, can safeguard it from unauthorized access.

Session token expiration is a critical consideration for advanced session management. Tokens should have limited lifespans to reduce the risk of session hijacking. Implementing short-lived tokens that expire after a specific duration or after a single use adds an extra layer of security.

Implementing session monitoring and anomaly detection systems can provide real-time visibility into session activities. By continuously monitoring session traffic and comparing it to baseline behavior, organizations can quickly identify and respond to abnormal session activities.

Implementing session integrity checks can prevent tampering with session data. By including a cryptographic checksum or signature with session data, web applications can detect any unauthorized modifications to the session, rendering compromised sessions useless.

Implementing user device fingerprinting as part of session management can enhance security. Device fingerprinting techniques can help verify the authenticity of the device used to access a session. By comparing device characteristics, such as browser type, operating system, and screen resolution, web applications can detect suspicious login attempts from unfamiliar devices.

Session access auditing is a crucial component of advanced session management. Logging and auditing access to sensitive sessions can provide a detailed history of who accessed a session and when. These logs can be invaluable for investigating security incidents and ensuring accountability.

Implementing adaptive session controls can dynamically adjust session security based on risk factors. For example, if an unusual login attempt is detected, the application can require additional authentication steps or impose stricter session restrictions.

Implementing secure logout mechanisms is essential for session management. Logging out should invalidate the session on both the client and server sides, ensuring that the user cannot be re-authenticated using the same session identifier.

In summary, advanced session management techniques are essential for securing web applications against a wide range of session-related threats. These techniques include session regeneration, secure communication, session timeouts, protection against XSS attacks, secure cookies, RBAC, session logging and monitoring, session token rotation, session revocation, session persistence in distributed environments, session encryption, token expiration, session monitoring and anomaly detection, session integrity checks, user device fingerprinting, session access auditing, adaptive session controls, and secure logout mechanisms. By implementing these advanced techniques, organizations can bolster the security of their session management and protect user data from unauthorized access and misuse.

Chapter 4: Tackling Cross-Site Scripting (XSS) Head-On

Cross-Site Scripting (XSS) is a prevalent and potentially dangerous web application security vulnerability. XSS occurs when an attacker injects malicious scripts, typically written in JavaScript, into web pages viewed by other users. The injected scripts are then executed in the context of the victim's browser, allowing the attacker to steal sensitive information, manipulate page content, or perform actions on behalf of the victim. XSS is a client-side attack, meaning it targets the browser and the user's interaction with a web application.

There are three main types of XSS attacks: stored XSS, reflected XSS, and DOM-based XSS. Stored XSS occurs when the malicious script is permanently stored on a web server and served to users when they access a particular page or resource. Reflected XSS involves injecting the malicious script into a URL or form input, which is then reflected back to the user within the application's response. DOM-based XSS, on the other hand, takes place entirely on the client side and involves manipulating the Document Object Model (DOM) of a web page through JavaScript.

The impact of XSS vulnerabilities can be significant, as attackers can use them to steal user credentials, session tokens, or other sensitive information. They can also deface websites, redirect users to malicious sites, or perform actions on behalf of users without their consent. Furthermore, XSS attacks can lead to data breaches, reputation damage, and legal consequences for organizations that fail to protect against them.

To prevent XSS attacks, web developers must adopt secure coding practices. One fundamental defense is input validation, which ensures that user-provided data is free of malicious scripts. Input validation involves checking the data's content, format, and length to ensure it meets expected criteria. Developers should reject any input that doesn't adhere to these criteria.

Output encoding is another crucial mitigation technique. It involves encoding user-generated content before displaying it in a web page. Encoding ensures that the browser interprets content as data rather than executable scripts. This prevents the browser from executing any injected malicious code.

Content Security Policy (CSP) is a security header that can help prevent XSS attacks. CSP allows web developers to specify which sources of content are trusted and should be executed by the browser. By defining a strict CSP policy, developers can mitigate the risk of unauthorized scripts executing in the user's browser.

HTTP-only and Secure flags for cookies can help protect against session theft through XSS attacks. The HTTP-only flag prevents JavaScript from accessing cookies, while the Secure flag ensures that cookies are transmitted only over secure, encrypted connections.

Web application firewalls (WAFs) are security devices that can detect and block XSS attacks. WAFs analyze incoming traffic and look for patterns or behavior indicative of XSS attempts. They can help organizations mitigate XSS attacks in real-time, but they should not be the sole defense.

To assess and mitigate XSS vulnerabilities, web application security testing is essential. Regular security testing, including automated scanning and manual penetration testing, can identify and remediate vulnerabilities in a web application. Testing should cover all input fields, URLs, and areas where user-generated content is displayed.

Education and training are vital for developers and security teams. Awareness of the risks associated with XSS attacks and knowledge of secure coding practices can help prevent such vulnerabilities from being introduced or overlooked during development.

Intrusion detection and monitoring systems can provide real-time alerts when potential XSS attacks are detected. These systems analyze network traffic and can trigger alerts based on predefined patterns or anomalies.

Client-side security controls, such as Content Security Policy (CSP), can also help protect against XSS. CSP defines which sources of content are trusted and can be executed by the browser, reducing the risk of unauthorized scripts running.

Regularly patching and updating web application components, including libraries and frameworks, is essential to prevent known vulnerabilities from being exploited by attackers. Many XSS attacks target known vulnerabilities in third-party components.

Implementing proper session management practices can also help mitigate the impact of XSS attacks. By ensuring that session tokens and sensitive data are stored securely and handled correctly, organizations can reduce the risk of data breaches.

Consider leveraging security libraries and frameworks designed to prevent XSS attacks. These tools often come with built-in security features and can simplify the process of implementing secure coding practices.

In summary, Cross-Site Scripting (XSS) is a prevalent web application security vulnerability that can have severe consequences if not properly mitigated. XSS attacks occur when attackers inject malicious scripts into web pages viewed by other users, enabling them to steal data, manipulate content, or perform actions on behalf of victims. There are three main types of XSS attacks: stored XSS, reflected XSS, and DOM-based XSS. To defend against XSS, web developers must adopt secure coding practices, including input validation, output encoding, Content Security Policy (CSP), HTTP-only and Secure flags for cookies, and the use of web application firewalls (WAFs). Security testing, education, intrusion detection, and client-side security controls are also essential components of a robust XSS defense strategy. By implementing these measures, organizations can protect their web applications and users from the risks associated with XSS vulnerabilities.

Comprehensive XSS (Cross-Site Scripting) prevention methods are crucial for safeguarding web applications against this pervasive and potentially damaging vulnerability. XSS attacks occur when malicious scripts are injected into web pages and executed in the context of a victim's browser, often with the goal of stealing sensitive information or performing unauthorized actions on behalf of users. To effectively prevent XSS attacks, web developers and organizations must employ a multi-layered approach that addresses various attack vectors and scenarios.

Input validation plays a fundamental role in XSS prevention by ensuring that user-provided data is free of malicious scripts. Developers should validate input data for content, format, and length, rejecting any inputs that do not adhere to expected criteria. By filtering out potentially dangerous input, web applications can minimize the risk of XSS vulnerabilities.

Output encoding is another critical defense mechanism in the XSS prevention arsenal. Output encoding involves encoding user-generated content before rendering it in web pages. This process ensures that any content displayed is treated as plain text and not executable code. By encoding output, web applications can prevent the browser from interpreting injected malicious scripts.

Content Security Policy (CSP) is a security header that helps prevent XSS attacks by specifying which sources of content are trusted and allowed to be executed by the browser. CSP policies define a set of rules that restrict the types of content that can be loaded and executed on a web page. By implementing a strict CSP policy, organizations can reduce the risk of unauthorized scripts running in the user's browser.

Using secure cookies is essential for preventing session theft through XSS attacks. Cookies that store session identifiers and other sensitive information should have the HttpOnly and Secure flags set. The HttpOnly flag prevents JavaScript from accessing cookies, while the Secure flag ensures that cookies are transmitted only over secure, encrypted connections.

Web application firewalls (WAFs) are security devices that can detect and block XSS attacks in real-time. WAFs analyze incoming web traffic and identify patterns or behavior indicative of XSS attempts. While WAFs can provide an additional layer of protection, they should not be relied upon as the sole defense against XSS.

Session management practices are integral to XSS prevention. Web applications should securely store and manage session tokens and sensitive data. Implementing secure session handling techniques ensures that attackers cannot easily hijack or manipulate user sessions.

Client-side security controls, such as CSP, can help protect against XSS by restricting which sources of content can be executed in the browser. These controls provide an extra layer of defense against malicious scripts and unauthorized code execution.

Regular security testing is a vital component of comprehensive XSS prevention. Web applications should undergo regular security assessments, including automated scanning and manual penetration testing, to identify and remediate vulnerabilities. Testing should encompass all input fields, URLs, and areas where user-generated content is displayed.

Education and training are essential for developers and security teams. Awareness of the risks associated with XSS attacks and knowledge of secure coding practices can help prevent vulnerabilities from being introduced or overlooked during development.

Intrusion detection and monitoring systems can provide real-time alerts when potential XSS attacks are detected. These systems analyze network traffic and trigger alerts based on predefined patterns or anomalies, allowing for swift responses to potential threats.

Implementing patch management practices is critical for preventing known vulnerabilities from being exploited by attackers. Web application components, including libraries and frameworks, should be regularly updated to address known security issues.

Leveraging security libraries and frameworks designed to prevent XSS attacks can simplify the process of implementing secure coding practices. These tools often come with built-in security features that can help protect against XSS vulnerabilities.

In summary, comprehensive XSS prevention methods are essential for protecting web applications and their users from the risks associated with this common and potentially damaging vulnerability. XSS attacks can lead to data breaches, reputation damage, and legal consequences for organizations that fail to address them effectively. To mitigate the threat of XSS, web developers and organizations should employ input validation, output encoding, Content Security Policy (CSP), secure cookies, web application firewalls (WAFs), session management practices, client-side security controls, security testing, education and training, intrusion detection, patch management, and security libraries and frameworks. By implementing these measures, organizations can significantly reduce the risk of XSS vulnerabilities and enhance the security of their web applications.

Chapter 5: Mastering Insecure Direct Object References

Insecure Direct Object References (IDOR) are a class of security vulnerabilities that occur when an application allows an attacker to manipulate object references, such as file names or database keys, in an unauthorized way. These vulnerabilities can lead to unauthorized access to sensitive data or functionality within an application. Understanding the advanced insights into IDOR vulnerabilities and how to mitigate them is crucial for maintaining the security of web applications.

One key aspect of IDOR vulnerabilities is the manipulation of object references in a way that allows an attacker to access resources or perform actions that should be restricted. For example, an attacker might change a URL parameter to access another user's private data or modify a value to gain administrative privileges. These vulnerabilities often arise from insufficient or improper access control mechanisms.

To mitigate IDOR vulnerabilities, developers must implement strong access control measures that ensure users can only access the data or functionality they are authorized to. Access control should be enforced both on the server-side and the client-side to prevent unauthorized requests from being executed. Developers should follow the principle of least privilege, granting users the minimum level of access necessary for their tasks.

It's essential to remember that client-side controls, such as hiding elements or disabling buttons, are not sufficient to prevent IDOR attacks. Attackers can easily manipulate client-side code, so access control must be enforced on the server. Access control checks should be performed for every request, regardless of whether it is initiated by a user action or an API call.

A common source of IDOR vulnerabilities is the improper use of object references, such as sequential integers or predictable values, as identifiers. Developers should avoid using easily guessable or sequential values as object references, as attackers can easily iterate through them to find unauthorized resources. Instead, use randomized or cryptographically secure identifiers that are difficult for attackers to predict.

Data validation and input validation are essential components of IDOR prevention. User-supplied data, such as input parameters, should be validated and sanitized to ensure it does not contain malicious or unauthorized references. For example, if a user inputs a file name, the application should validate that the file exists and that the user has the necessary permissions to access it.

Session management plays a crucial role in IDOR prevention. Sessions should be securely managed, and session tokens should not be exposed in URLs or other insecure locations. Implementing proper session timeouts and authentication mechanisms can reduce the risk of session-based IDOR attacks.

Access control lists (ACLs) and role-based access control (RBAC) are advanced techniques that can enhance access control and prevent IDOR vulnerabilities. ACLs allow fine-grained control over which users or roles can access specific resources or perform certain actions. RBAC assigns users to roles, and each role has a defined set of permissions, ensuring that users only have access to authorized functionality.

APIs are often vulnerable to IDOR attacks, as they expose endpoints that may not have adequate access controls. Developers should implement strong access controls for API endpoints and ensure that authorization checks are performed for every API request. Rate limiting and authentication tokens can also help protect APIs from IDOR attacks.

Regular security testing, including manual testing and automated scanning, is essential to identify and remediate IDOR vulnerabilities. Security assessments should include testing for IDOR issues, such as trying to access resources that should be restricted. Additionally, thorough code reviews can help detect insecure object reference code patterns.

User education and awareness are essential for preventing IDOR vulnerabilities. Users should be educated about the importance of not tampering with URLs or request parameters to access unauthorized resources. Implementing mechanisms to detect and report suspicious activities, such as repeated failed access attempts, can also help mitigate IDOR risks.

In summary, gaining advanced insights into Insecure Direct Object References (IDOR) vulnerabilities is crucial for web application security. IDOR vulnerabilities occur when attackers manipulate object references to gain unauthorized access to resources or functionality. Mitigating IDOR vulnerabilities requires strong access control measures, data validation, session management, and the use of secure identifiers. Advanced techniques, such as access control lists (ACLs) and role-based access control (RBAC), can enhance access control. APIs should also be protected from IDOR attacks, and regular security testing and user education are vital components of IDOR prevention. By understanding and addressing these aspects, developers and organizations can significantly reduce the risk of IDOR vulnerabilities in their web applications.

Fine-tuning access control and authorization is a critical aspect of web application security, ensuring that users are granted precisely the level of access they need and no more. Properly configuring access control mechanisms helps prevent unauthorized access to sensitive data and functionality, reducing the risk of security breaches. Fine-tuning access control involves implementing granular access controls, enforcing strong authentication, and continuously monitoring and adjusting permissions to align with changing requirements.

Granular access controls involve breaking down access permissions into small, specific components. Rather than granting or denying access to an entire resource or feature, fine-tuned access controls allow administrators to define precisely which actions a user or role can perform. This granularity minimizes the risk of over-privileged users and limits the potential impact of security incidents.

Role-based access control (RBAC) is a widely used approach for fine-tuning access control. RBAC assigns users to roles, and each role is associated with a set of permissions or privileges. By defining roles based on job functions or responsibilities, organizations can ensure that users are granted only the necessary permissions for their tasks. RBAC simplifies access control management and reduces the risk of misconfigurations.

Attribute-based access control (ABAC) is another advanced method for fine-tuning access control. ABAC considers a wide range of attributes, such as user attributes, resource attributes, and environmental attributes, to make access decisions. This approach allows organizations to create highly dynamic and context-aware access control policies. For example, access to a document could be determined based on the user's department, the document's classification, and the user's location.

Strong authentication mechanisms are essential for fine-tuning access control. Multi-factor authentication (MFA) and biometric authentication provide additional layers of security beyond traditional username and password combinations. By requiring multiple forms of authentication, organizations can further verify the identity of users before granting access to sensitive resources.

Continuous monitoring and adjustment of access control permissions are vital for maintaining security. Access control should not be a one-time setup; instead, it should be an ongoing process. Organizations should regularly review access permissions, evaluate their relevance, and adjust them as needed. This includes revoking access when users change roles or responsibilities.

Audit trails and logs play a crucial role in fine-tuning access control. Logging access control events allows organizations to track who accessed what resources and when. Logs can be used for auditing, compliance, and incident response purposes. Monitoring access logs for suspicious activities helps organizations identify and address security threats promptly.

Access control testing is an essential part of fine-tuning. Organizations should perform penetration testing and security assessments to identify vulnerabilities and misconfigurations in access control mechanisms. Regular testing helps ensure that access controls are effective and aligned with security policies.

Delegation of authority is another aspect of fine-tuning access control. Organizations should have processes in place to delegate access control responsibilities to specific individuals or teams. This delegation should be done carefully, with clear guidelines and accountability, to avoid over-privileged users or insecure configurations.

Access control documentation is critical for maintaining a clear and well-documented access control policy. Documentation should include details about roles, permissions, access control rules, and the rationale behind them. Having up-to-date documentation helps ensure that access controls are consistent and aligned with the organization's security objectives.

Cloud-based and remote access control require special attention in today's digital landscape. Organizations should implement access controls that are suitable for remote and cloud environments, considering factors like authentication, encryption, and secure protocols. Fine-tuning access control for remote access helps organizations secure their data and resources in an increasingly mobile and distributed world.

Access control policies should be aligned with the principle of least privilege (PoLP). PoLP dictates that users or roles should be granted the minimum level of access necessary to perform their duties. By adhering to PoLP, organizations can reduce the attack surface and limit the potential impact of security incidents.

Regular access control reviews and audits are essential for fine-tuning. Organizations should conduct periodic reviews of access controls, focusing on identifying over-privileged users or roles. Audits can uncover misconfigurations or discrepancies in access control policies.

Collaboration between IT, security teams, and business units is critical for fine-tuning access control. Clear communication and understanding of business requirements help ensure that access controls are aligned with organizational goals. Security teams should work closely with business units to define access control requirements accurately.

In summary, fine-tuning access control and authorization is a crucial aspect of web application security. Granular access controls, RBAC, ABAC, strong authentication, continuous monitoring, and adjustment of permissions are essential components of a robust access control strategy. Regular testing, delegation of authority, documentation, and alignment with PoLP principles further enhance access control. In today's digital landscape, remote and cloud-based access control considerations are vital for securing data and resources. Collaboration between IT, security teams, and business units ensures that access controls meet the organization's security objectives and business needs. By fine-tuning access control, organizations can minimize the risk of unauthorized access and strengthen their overall security posture.

Chapter 6: Fine-Tuning Security Configurations

Optimizing web application security configurations is a critical step in enhancing the overall security posture of an application. Security configurations encompass a wide range of settings and parameters that determine how a web application operates and how it handles potential security threats. By fine-tuning these configurations, organizations can reduce vulnerabilities, mitigate risks, and improve the resilience of their web applications.

One key aspect of optimizing web application security configurations is ensuring that the application follows security best practices and industry standards. This includes adhering to guidelines such as those provided by the Open Web Application Security Project (OWASP) and the Center for Internet Security (CIS). These organizations offer valuable resources and recommendations for securing web applications, and following their guidance can significantly enhance security.

A crucial element of security configurations is the proper management of authentication and authorization mechanisms. Authentication ensures that users are who they claim to be, while authorization determines what actions users are allowed to perform. Organizations should implement strong authentication methods, such as multi-factor authentication (MFA), and enforce least privilege principles to limit access to authorized users.

Securing sensitive data is another important consideration in web application security configurations. Encrypting data both in transit and at rest helps protect it from unauthorized access. Organizations should use secure encryption protocols and algorithms and regularly update encryption keys to maintain data security.

Web server and application server configurations play a vital role in security. Disabling unnecessary services and features, applying security patches promptly, and hardening server settings can reduce the attack surface and prevent common vulnerabilities. Organizations should also implement secure HTTP headers to protect against various types of attacks, such as cross-site scripting (XSS) and clickjacking.

Input validation and output encoding are essential security configurations that protect against injection attacks, such as SQL injection and cross-site scripting. Input validation ensures that user-provided data meets expected criteria, while output encoding ensures that data is displayed as plain text, preventing the execution of malicious scripts. Organizations should implement strict input validation and output encoding routines for all user inputs and outputs.

File and resource access controls are crucial security configurations to prevent unauthorized access to sensitive files or directories. Organizations should implement access controls, such as proper file permissions, to restrict access to authorized users and deny access to unauthenticated or unauthorized individuals. Additionally, organizations should avoid exposing sensitive information, such as configuration files or database credentials, in publicly accessible locations.

Web application firewalls (WAFs) are security tools that can be integrated into the security configurations to provide an additional layer of protection. WAFs inspect incoming web traffic and can detect and block various types of attacks, including SQL injection, XSS, and cross-site request forgery (CSRF). However, organizations should configure WAFs carefully to avoid false positives and ensure that legitimate traffic is not blocked.

Session management settings are vital for protecting user sessions from attacks like session fixation or session hijacking. Organizations should use secure session management techniques, such as generating random session identifiers, implementing session timeouts, and securely transmitting session tokens. Additionally, session management settings should be configured to revoke or invalidate sessions after logout to prevent unauthorized access.

Error handling and logging configurations should be fine-tuned to prevent the disclosure of sensitive information in error messages. Error messages should provide minimal details to users and log detailed error information for administrators. Organizations should monitor error logs regularly to detect and address potential security issues.

Content Security Policy (CSP) is a powerful security configuration that helps prevent cross-site scripting (XSS) attacks by specifying which sources of content are trusted and allowed to be executed by the browser. Implementing a strict CSP policy can significantly reduce the risk of unauthorized scripts running in the user's browser.

Regular security testing, including automated scanning and manual penetration testing, is essential for verifying the effectiveness of security configurations. Testing helps identify vulnerabilities and misconfigurations that may have been overlooked during the configuration process. Security assessments should cover all aspects of the web application, including authentication, authorization, input validation, output encoding, and session management.

Continuous monitoring is a critical part of optimizing web application security configurations. Organizations should continuously monitor security logs, traffic patterns, and potential security incidents. Monitoring helps identify suspicious activities and allows organizations to respond promptly to security threats.

Regularly updating security configurations is essential to adapt to evolving threats and vulnerabilities. Organizations should stay informed about security updates and patches for web application components, including web servers, application servers, libraries, and frameworks. Updating configurations to align with the latest security recommendations and patches helps maintain the security of the application.

In summary, optimizing web application security configurations is a crucial aspect of web application security. Security configurations encompass various settings and parameters that determine how an application operates and handles security threats. By following security best practices, managing authentication and authorization, securing sensitive data, and configuring web and application servers, organizations can reduce vulnerabilities and mitigate risks. Implementing input validation, output encoding, access controls, and secure session management further enhances security. Utilizing security tools like web application firewalls (WAFs) and Content Security Policy (CSP) can provide additional layers of protection. Regular security testing, monitoring, and updates ensure that security configurations remain effective in protecting web applications from evolving threats.

Implementing security policies effectively is a critical aspect of safeguarding an organization's information assets and ensuring the overall security posture. Security policies are a set of documented guidelines and rules that define the security practices and expectations within an organization. These policies provide a framework for decision-making, help manage risk, and guide employees, contractors, and partners on how to protect sensitive data and resources.

The first step in implementing security policies effectively is to establish a clear and comprehensive set of policies that cover all aspects of the organization's operations. These policies should be tailored to the organization's specific needs and risks and should align with industry standards and regulations. A well-drafted policy provides a solid foundation for security efforts.

Security policies must be communicated to all employees, contractors, and relevant stakeholders within the organization. Clear communication ensures that everyone understands their responsibilities, the rules they need to follow, and the consequences of non-compliance. Training and awareness programs are essential to reinforce the importance of security policies and educate individuals on how to adhere to them.

Assigning ownership and responsibility for security policies is crucial. A designated individual or team should be responsible for overseeing and enforcing the policies. This includes monitoring compliance, conducting audits, and addressing violations or incidents promptly. Clear lines of responsibility help ensure that policies are not merely documents but are actively enforced.

Implementing security policies effectively requires a risk assessment process to identify vulnerabilities and threats to the organization. This assessment helps organizations prioritize their security efforts and allocate resources where they are most needed. Security policies should be tailored to address the specific risks identified in the assessment.

Regular reviews and updates of security policies are necessary to keep them relevant and effective. The threat landscape is constantly evolving, and technologies change rapidly. Policies should be reviewed at least annually and updated as needed to address new risks or emerging technologies. This ensures that security practices remain aligned with the organization's goals and risks.

Enforcement of security policies is a critical aspect of implementation. Policies should specify consequences for non-compliance, which may include disciplinary actions or sanctions. Enforcement should be consistent and applied fairly across all levels of the organization, including senior leadership.

Monitoring and auditing are essential components of effective policy implementation. Organizations should regularly assess compliance with security policies through audits, reviews, and assessments. These processes help identify areas of non-compliance or weaknesses in policy enforcement that need to be addressed.

Security policies should be integrated into the organization's culture and daily operations. This means that security should be considered in all decision-making processes, from design and development to procurement and operations. Security awareness should become a part of the organization's DNA, with employees and stakeholders actively thinking about security in their roles. Implementing security policies effectively involves providing resources and tools to support compliance. This may include security software, training programs, access control systems, and incident response procedures. Providing the necessary resources empowers individuals to follow the policies and maintain a secure environment.

Security policies should align with legal and regulatory requirements. Organizations must ensure that their policies meet the legal obligations and compliance standards relevant to their industry. Failure to comply with these requirements can result in legal consequences and damage to the organization's reputation.

Creating a culture of accountability is essential for effective policy implementation. Individuals should understand that security is everyone's responsibility, from the CEO to the newest employee. Fostering a culture of accountability ensures that security policies are not seen as burdensome but as essential for protecting the organization.

Regular communication and training are essential for keeping security policies top of mind. Organizations should provide ongoing education to employees and stakeholders, helping them understand the importance of security policies and how to comply with them. Regular reminders and updates help reinforce the policies' importance.

Security policies should be accessible and easy to understand. Complex and lengthy policies are less likely to be followed. Organizations should strive to create concise, clear, and user-friendly policies that individuals can reference easily when needed.

Implementing security policies effectively involves continuous improvement. Organizations should learn from incidents and security breaches and use these experiences to refine and enhance their policies. Security should be a dynamic and evolving aspect of the organization's culture.

Security policies should cover all aspects of the organization's operations, including data protection, access control, incident response, and disaster recovery. Each policy should be tailored to address specific risks and threats relevant to the organization's environment and industry. By having comprehensive policies in place, organizations can mitigate a wide range of security risks.

In summary, implementing security policies effectively is essential for protecting an organization's information assets and ensuring a strong security posture. This process involves creating clear and comprehensive policies, communicating them to all stakeholders, assigning responsibility for enforcement, conducting regular assessments, and integrating security into the organization's culture and daily operations. Regular reviews and updates, along with consistent enforcement, help maintain the relevance and effectiveness of security policies. A culture of accountability, ongoing education, and accessibility of policies contribute to successful implementation. Ultimately, security policies play a crucial role in safeguarding an organization from evolving threats and risks in the digital age.

Chapter 7: Advanced Defense Against Cross-Site Request Forgery (CSRF)

Understanding advanced CSRF (Cross-Site Request Forgery) attack scenarios is essential for web application security professionals and developers tasked with safeguarding applications from this prevalent threat. While basic CSRF attacks involve tricking a user into executing unauthorized actions, advanced CSRF attacks leverage more sophisticated techniques to evade detection and cause substantial damage. Next, we will delve into some advanced CSRF attack scenarios, explore their intricacies, and discuss mitigation strategies to protect web applications effectively.

One advanced CSRF attack scenario is the "Blind CSRF" or "Invisible CSRF" attack. In this scenario, an attacker crafts a malicious payload that forces the victim to perform actions without the victim's knowledge. Unlike traditional CSRF attacks, where the victim must be tricked into clicking a malicious link or visiting a malicious website, Blind CSRF attacks occur without the user's active involvement.

The Blind CSRF attack typically relies on vulnerabilities in the victim's browser, such as insecurely configured cross-origin requests. For example, modern browsers have mechanisms like Same-Origin Policy (SOP) to prevent cross-origin requests initiated by malicious websites. However, if a web application doesn't properly implement SOP or has security misconfigurations, it may allow cross-origin requests initiated by an attacker-controlled site.

In a Blind CSRF attack, the attacker hosts a malicious website that contains crafted code to send unauthorized requests to the target web application. When the victim visits the attacker's site, their browser executes the malicious code, sending requests to the target application on the victim's behalf. Since the requests originate from the victim's browser, they may be treated as legitimate by the target application.

Blind CSRF attacks can be particularly challenging to detect, as the victim remains unaware of the malicious actions taking place. To mitigate Blind CSRF attacks, web developers should implement strict cross-origin request policies, including using appropriate headers like Cross-Origin Resource Sharing (CORS). Additionally, employing anti-CSRF tokens and implementing strong session management practices can help prevent these attacks.

Another advanced CSRF attack scenario is the "Double Submit Cookie" attack. In this scenario, the attacker crafts a malicious web page that tricks the victim into performing actions on a target application, leveraging the application's reliance on cookies for session management. The attacker embeds malicious JavaScript code in the web page, which sends forged requests containing both the victim's cookies and the malicious payload. When the victim visits the attacker's page, their browser executes the malicious code, sending requests with the victim's authentication cookies to the target application. The target application, relying solely on cookies for session identification, may interpret these requests as legitimate and execute the actions specified in the payload.

Mitigating Double Submit Cookie attacks involves implementing additional security measures, such as using anti-CSRF tokens. These tokens should be generated and verified on the server-side for every sensitive action. Since cookies alone are insufficient for preventing CSRF attacks, the use of anti-CSRF tokens adds an extra layer of protection against such threats. A more sophisticated CSRF attack scenario is the "Cross-Site WebSocket Hijacking" attack. In this scenario, the attacker targets web applications that use WebSocket connections for real-time communication. WebSocket is a protocol that allows two-way communication between a web application and a server, and it is increasingly popular for modern web applications.

To execute a Cross-Site WebSocket Hijacking attack, the attacker crafts a malicious web page containing JavaScript code designed to open WebSocket connections to a target application. If the target application lacks proper WebSocket security measures, it may accept and maintain these connections without verifying the source.

Once the WebSocket connection is established, the attacker can initiate WebSocket messages that trigger actions on the target application. Since WebSocket connections can persist, the attacker can continue to exploit the connection to perform unauthorized actions as long as the WebSocket session remains open.

Mitigating Cross-Site WebSocket Hijacking attacks requires careful implementation of WebSocket security. Developers should ensure that WebSocket connections are authenticated, authorized, and properly encrypted. Additionally, the use of anti-CSRF tokens and secure session management remains crucial to prevent these advanced attacks.

The "XMLHttpRequest CSRF" attack is another advanced CSRF scenario. In this attack, the attacker leverages the XMLHttpRequest object, a standard JavaScript API for making HTTP requests from a web page. Typically used for asynchronous communication, this object can be exploited if the target application doesn't validate the origin of incoming requests properly.

To execute an XMLHttpRequest CSRF attack, the attacker crafts a web page containing JavaScript code that sends malicious XMLHttpRequests to the target application. These requests may include actions that, when executed, can result in undesirable consequences for the victim.

The main challenge in mitigating XMLHttpRequest CSRF attacks is ensuring that the application correctly validates the origin of incoming requests. Developers should implement server-side checks to verify that the request's origin matches an approved list of domains or follows a secure cross-origin request policy. By validating request origins, applications can prevent XMLHttpRequest CSRF attacks.

Lastly, an advanced CSRF attack scenario known as "Cross-Origin Read Blocking" (CORB) bypass exploits a browser feature designed to protect against data theft. CORB is intended to block potentially sensitive data from being read by malicious websites. However, attackers have found ways to bypass CORB protections.

In a CORB bypass attack, the attacker crafts a web page that requests sensitive data from a target application. By leveraging various techniques, such as abusing the way browsers handle certain content types or manipulating the response headers, the attacker tricks the browser into delivering the protected data to their malicious web page.

Mitigating CORB bypass attacks requires understanding the intricacies of browser security mechanisms and staying informed about browser updates and patches. Developers should follow best practices for response header configuration, content type handling, and implementing security controls to prevent unauthorized data access. To effectively defend against advanced Cross-Site Request Forgery (CSRF) attacks, it's essential to employ advanced defense strategies that go beyond basic measures. While basic CSRF defenses like using anti-CSRF tokens and implementing Same-Site cookies provide a solid foundation, advanced attackers can exploit vulnerabilities in more sophisticated ways. Next, we will explore advanced CSRF defense strategies that can help protect web applications from these complex threats.

One advanced defense strategy is to implement a "Referer Policy." The Referer Policy is an HTTP header that controls how a browser shares the referring URL when a user navigates from one page to another. By configuring the Referer Policy, web developers can restrict the information disclosed in the HTTP Referer header, thereby reducing the risk of CSRF attacks.

To implement a Referer Policy, developers can set specific directives in the HTTP headers of their web applications. For example, setting the "strict-origin" directive ensures that the Referer header is only sent when navigating from one page on the same origin (i.e., the same domain and protocol). This prevents malicious websites from learning the user's session cookies and launching CSRF attacks based on the Referer header.

Another advanced CSRF defense strategy involves "Same-Site Cookies" with the "Strict" attribute. Same-Site Cookies are designed to prevent cookies from being sent in cross-site requests, which is crucial for mitigating CSRF attacks. By using the "Strict" attribute when setting cookies, developers can ensure that cookies are only sent when the request originates from the same site.

To enable the "Strict" attribute for cookies, developers can include it when defining or setting cookies in their web applications. This attribute instructs the browser to restrict the cookie's scope to the same origin, effectively blocking CSRF attacks that rely on cookies sent with malicious requests from other sites.

Implementing Content Security Policy (CSP) is an advanced defense strategy that can mitigate various web security risks, including CSRF attacks. CSP is an HTTP header that controls which resources are allowed to be loaded and executed by a web page. Developers can specify which domains and content sources are trusted, preventing the execution of unauthorized scripts or requests.

To configure CSP, developers need to define a CSP policy in the HTTP header of their web application. The policy can include directives such as "script-src" to specify trusted sources for JavaScript execution. By defining a strict CSP policy, developers can prevent the execution of malicious scripts, including those that attempt CSRF attacks.

The use of "Content-Type" headers is another advanced CSRF defense strategy. When handling incoming requests, web applications should validate the content type of the request body. By checking that the content type matches the expected type, applications can detect and reject CSRF requests that attempt to send unauthorized data.

For instance, if a web application expects JSON data in a POST request, it should validate that the "Content-Type" header of the request is set to "application/json." Any request with an unexpected or mismatched content type should be rejected, as it may be an attempt to exploit CSRF vulnerabilities. Implementing "Cross-Origin Resource Sharing" (CORS) with fine-grained control is an advanced CSRF defense strategy. CORS is a mechanism that allows or restricts web pages in one domain from making requests to resources hosted on another domain. By configuring CORS policies with fine-grained control, developers can specify which domains are allowed to make cross-origin requests to their web applications.

To implement fine-grained CORS control, developers can set specific CORS headers in their web application responses. These headers can include "Access-Control-Allow-Origin," "Access-Control-Allow-Methods," and "Access-Control-Allow-Headers" to define the allowed origins, HTTP methods, and headers for cross-origin requests. By restricting access to trusted domains, developers can mitigate the risk of CSRF attacks from unauthorized sources.

Implementing "Origin Validation" is an advanced defense strategy that focuses on validating the "Origin" header of incoming requests. The "Origin" header indicates the source of an HTTP request, helping web applications determine whether the request is from a trusted origin. By validating the "Origin" header, applications can reject requests from untrusted or unauthorized sources.

Developers can implement "Origin Validation" by checking the "Origin" header of incoming requests and comparing it to a list of trusted origins. If the "Origin" header does not match any of the trusted origins, the request should be rejected, as it may be an attempt to exploit CSRF vulnerabilities.

The use of "Double Submit Cookies" is an advanced CSRF defense strategy that involves binding cookies to specific user actions. In this approach, a unique, random anti-CSRF token is embedded in both a cookie and a form field. When a user submits a form, the web application checks whether the token in the cookie matches the token in the form field. If they match, the request is considered valid; otherwise, it is rejected.

Implementing "Double Submit Cookies" requires developers to generate and manage unique tokens for each user session and associate them with user actions. This strategy ensures that even if an attacker manages to include a malicious token in a CSRF attack, it will not match the token in the user's cookie.

A comprehensive defense strategy against advanced CSRF attacks should include regular security testing and vulnerability assessments. Developers should conduct thorough security assessments, including penetration testing and code reviews, to identify and address potential CSRF vulnerabilities in their web applications. Regular testing helps ensure that the implemented defense strategies remain effective and adapt to evolving threats.

In summary, defending against advanced CSRF attacks requires web developers to implement a combination of advanced defense strategies. These strategies include configuring Referer Policies, using Same-Site Cookies with the "Strict" attribute, implementing Content Security Policy (CSP), checking "Content-Type" headers, configuring fine-grained CORS policies, validating "Origin" headers, and utilizing Double Submit Cookies. Regular security testing and vulnerability assessments are essential to maintain the effectiveness of these defense mechanisms and protect web applications from sophisticated CSRF threats.

Chapter 8: Managing Components with Known Vulnerabilities

Managing vulnerable components in a complex software ecosystem presents numerous challenges that organizations must address to maintain a secure and robust environment. One of the primary challenges is the sheer volume of components that modern applications rely on. Many software projects depend on numerous third-party libraries, frameworks, and modules, each with its own set of dependencies. Keeping track of these components and their vulnerabilities can be a daunting task.

Another challenge is the rapid pace at which vulnerabilities are discovered and disclosed. The software industry's vibrant open-source community constantly identifies and reports security flaws in various components. This means that organizations must continuously monitor and assess their software stack for newly discovered vulnerabilities.

Prioritizing which vulnerabilities to address first can also be a significant challenge. Not all vulnerabilities are created equal, and organizations need to determine which ones pose the most significant risk to their applications. This requires a careful assessment of the potential impact and exploitability of each vulnerability in the context of their specific environment.

Additionally, the lack of awareness and visibility into the components used in a project can be problematic. Developers may unknowingly introduce vulnerable components into their applications when they include third-party code. Without a comprehensive inventory of components, it becomes challenging to track and remediate vulnerabilities effectively.

Managing vulnerable components across a large and diverse software portfolio can lead to resource constraints. Organizations may struggle to allocate enough time, personnel, and financial resources to address all identified vulnerabilities promptly. This can result in delays in addressing critical issues, leaving applications exposed to potential attacks.

Another challenge is the complexity of coordinating efforts across development teams, operations teams, and security teams. Effective component management requires collaboration and communication among these groups, but siloed workflows and differing priorities can hinder the process.

Furthermore, legacy systems and outdated software can pose significant challenges in terms of component management. Some organizations may have applications running on old technologies or unsupported platforms, making it difficult to find patches or updates for vulnerable components.

The risk of introducing new vulnerabilities during the patching process is a concern. When organizations rush to fix known vulnerabilities, they may inadvertently introduce other issues or break existing functionality. This risk underscores the importance of thorough testing and quality assurance during the remediation process.

Vendor dependency can also be a challenge, as organizations rely on software vendors to provide updates and patches for components they supply. If a vendor is slow to address vulnerabilities or discontinues support for a component, organizations may find themselves in a precarious situation.

Effective component management requires a well-defined process and policy framework. Organizations need clear guidelines on how to assess, prioritize, and remediate vulnerabilities. Lack of such a framework can result in inconsistent practices and delays in addressing security issues.

The lack of standardized vulnerability databases and scoring systems can complicate the assessment of component vulnerabilities. Different databases may report the same vulnerability with varying severity ratings, making it challenging to prioritize remediation efforts accurately.

Organizations also face challenges related to visibility into the supply chain of components. Knowing the origin and security posture of third-party components is crucial, as vulnerabilities may be introduced during the development or distribution process.

Furthermore, the lack of automated tools for vulnerability detection and remediation can slow down the process. Organizations need robust scanning and analysis tools to identify and assess vulnerabilities in their software stack efficiently.

Finally, keeping up with compliance requirements and industry regulations adds another layer of complexity to component management. Organizations in regulated industries must ensure that their software meets specific security and compliance standards, which may require additional effort and resources.

In summary, managing vulnerable components in software applications is a multifaceted challenge that organizations must navigate to maintain a secure and resilient software ecosystem. The challenges include the volume of components, the rapid discovery of vulnerabilities, prioritization difficulties, awareness and visibility issues, resource constraints, coordination complexities, legacy systems, patching risks, vendor dependencies, process and policy frameworks, database inconsistencies, supply chain concerns, automation needs, and compliance requirements. Addressing these challenges requires a holistic approach that combines technology, processes, and collaboration to effectively mitigate the risks associated with vulnerable components and ensure the security of software applications.

Chapter 9: Advanced Web Application Security Testing

In the ever-evolving landscape of software development, advanced approaches to component security are essential to mitigate the risks associated with vulnerable components and ensure the integrity of software applications. One advanced approach is the use of Software Composition Analysis (SCA) tools that provide comprehensive visibility into the components used within a software project. SCA tools automatically detect and inventory dependencies, providing developers and security teams with an up-to-date list of components and their versions.

These tools also help organizations monitor for security vulnerabilities in their component dependencies by continuously scanning public databases and repositories. Additionally, SCA tools can categorize vulnerabilities by severity, making it easier for organizations to prioritize remediation efforts. By incorporating SCA into the development pipeline, organizations can proactively identify and address vulnerabilities before they become security incidents.

Another advanced approach to component security is the establishment of a robust Software Bill of Materials (SBOM). An SBOM is a detailed inventory of all components and dependencies used in a software application, including their version numbers and sources. This document provides transparency into the software supply chain, helping organizations trace the origin of each component and assess its security posture.

By creating an SBOM, organizations can quickly identify vulnerable components, track their usage across projects, and make informed decisions about their inclusion in future software development efforts. An SBOM also facilitates compliance with industry regulations and standards that require transparency in software supply chains.

Organizations can enhance component security by adopting a Zero Trust approach. Zero Trust assumes that no component, whether internal or external, is inherently trustworthy. Instead, it requires continuous verification of identities and strict access controls for components and users.

By implementing Zero Trust principles, organizations can minimize the attack surface and reduce the risk of vulnerabilities being exploited. This approach involves granular access controls, strong authentication mechanisms, and continuous monitoring of component interactions within a network.

Machine learning and artificial intelligence (AI) technologies can play a significant role in advanced component security. These technologies can be used to analyze and identify patterns of behavior and detect anomalies that may indicate security threats. For example, machine learning algorithms can monitor network traffic and identify suspicious activities or deviations from normal behavior, helping organizations detect and respond to security incidents in real-time.

Secure Development Lifecycle (SDL) practices should be enhanced with advanced security training and awareness programs. Developers and security teams should receive ongoing training to stay updated on the latest security threats and best practices. Furthermore, organizations can implement secure coding guidelines and automated code analysis tools to identify and address security vulnerabilities during the development process.

Another advanced approach is the use of threat modeling and risk assessments specific to component security. Organizations should conduct in-depth assessments to identify potential threats and vulnerabilities associated with each component. This allows for the development of tailored security controls and measures to mitigate these risks effectively.

Organizations can also leverage bug bounty programs and crowdsourced security testing to identify and remediate component vulnerabilities. By offering incentives to ethical hackers and security researchers, organizations can discover and address vulnerabilities before they are exploited by malicious actors.

Advanced approaches to component security should also involve ongoing monitoring and incident response capabilities. Security teams should have the tools and processes in place to detect and respond to security incidents related to component vulnerabilities promptly. This includes monitoring for active exploitation of known vulnerabilities and having incident response plans in place to contain and mitigate any breaches.

Additionally, organizations can benefit from threat intelligence feeds that provide real-time information on emerging threats and vulnerabilities. These feeds can help security teams stay ahead of potential attacks by providing timely alerts and actionable information.

In summary, advanced approaches to component security are crucial in today's software development landscape.

These approaches include the use of Software Composition Analysis (SCA) tools, establishing a Software Bill of Materials (SBOM), adopting a Zero Trust approach, leveraging machine learning and AI, enhancing secure development practices, conducting threat modeling and risk assessments, implementing bug bounty programs, and establishing ongoing monitoring and incident response capabilities. By embracing these advanced approaches, organizations can better protect their software applications from component-related vulnerabilities and maintain a strong security posture in an ever-changing threat environment.

Creating a comprehensive security testing plan is a critical step in ensuring the security of software applications and systems. Such a plan serves as a roadmap for identifying vulnerabilities, assessing risks, and implementing security controls throughout the development lifecycle. To create an effective security testing plan, it's essential to consider various factors and follow best practices.

The first step in creating a security testing plan is to define the scope and objectives of the testing effort. This involves determining which parts of the application or system will be tested, the specific security goals, and the desired outcomes. A clear and well-defined scope helps in allocating resources and setting expectations.

Next, identify the types of security tests that need to be conducted. These tests can include vulnerability assessments, penetration testing, code reviews, and security scanning. Each type of test focuses on different aspects of security and helps uncover various types of vulnerabilities.

Once the types of tests are identified, it's crucial to select appropriate tools and methodologies for each. Consider the technology stack, programming languages, and frameworks used in the application, as these factors may influence the choice of testing tools and approaches. Using a combination of automated and manual testing methods can provide comprehensive coverage.

Define the frequency and timing of security testing activities. Regular testing throughout the development lifecycle, including during design, development, and post-deployment phases, is essential. This ensures that security is considered at every stage and vulnerabilities are addressed promptly.

Allocate resources, including personnel and tools, for conducting security tests. Identify the roles and responsibilities of team members involved in testing, such as security analysts, developers, and quality assurance professionals. Having a dedicated security testing team can help streamline the process and ensure thorough testing.

Establish a testing environment that closely mirrors the production environment to simulate real-world scenarios. This includes using similar hardware, software configurations, and network setups. Testing in a controlled environment helps identify vulnerabilities that may not be apparent in isolated testing.

Create a set of test cases and scenarios that cover a wide range of security issues. These test cases should be based on known security best practices and potential threats. Include both common and specific test cases tailored to the application's unique features and functionality.

Consider compliance requirements and industry standards when defining test cases. Ensure that the application aligns with relevant regulations, such as GDPR, HIPAA, or PCI DSS, if applicable. Compliance-focused test cases help demonstrate adherence to legal and industry-specific security standards.

Include threat modeling as part of the security testing plan. Threat modeling involves identifying potential threats, their impacts, and possible mitigation strategies. It helps prioritize security efforts and ensures that testing addresses the most critical risks.

Implement continuous testing and integration into the development pipeline. Integrate security testing tools and processes into the build and deployment pipeline to catch vulnerabilities early. Automated testing can be triggered with each code commit or deployment, ensuring that security checks are part of the development workflow.

Establish clear criteria for evaluating test results. Define what constitutes a security issue, its severity, and the steps to reproduce it. Having predefined criteria ensures consistency in evaluating vulnerabilities and helps prioritize remediation efforts.

Plan for remediation and follow-up actions for identified vulnerabilities. Create a process for reporting and tracking security issues, assigning them to the responsible parties, and monitoring their resolution. Ensure that vulnerabilities are addressed in a timely manner to minimize risk.

Consider the scalability of the security testing plan. As the application evolves and grows, the testing plan should adapt to accommodate changes. Regularly review and update the plan to incorporate new technologies, features, and potential threats.

Include measures for security awareness and training. Ensure that team members involved in development and testing receive ongoing training on security best practices and emerging threats. A well-informed team is better equipped to identify and address security issues.

Perform a final review of the security testing plan before implementation. Validate that all aspects of the plan align with the project's goals and requirements. Address any gaps or inconsistencies and ensure that the plan is ready for execution.

Execute the security testing plan according to the defined schedule and scope. Regularly monitor the progress of testing activities and adjust the plan as needed based on emerging findings and priorities.

Upon completion of testing, compile a comprehensive report that includes details of identified vulnerabilities, their severity, and recommended remediation steps. Share this report with relevant stakeholders, including developers, management, and security teams.

Engage in a debriefing and lessons learned session after testing. Review the testing process, outcomes, and any challenges encountered. Use this feedback to improve future security testing efforts and refine the testing plan.

In summary, creating a comprehensive security testing plan is essential for safeguarding software applications and systems against evolving security threats. By defining the scope and objectives, selecting appropriate testing methods, allocating resources, and integrating security testing into the development lifecycle, organizations can proactively identify and mitigate vulnerabilities. Regular updates and continuous improvement of the testing plan ensure that security remains a top priority throughout the software development process.

Chapter 10: Beyond the Top 10: Emerging Threats and Best Practices

As technology evolves, so do the threats that target web applications, and staying ahead of these new and emerging threats is critical for maintaining a secure online presence. Understanding the evolving landscape of web application threats is essential for organizations and security professionals. One of the emerging threats that has gained significant attention in recent years is the rise of sophisticated bot attacks. These bots, often powered by machine learning and AI, can mimic human behavior and evade traditional security measures.

Bot attacks encompass various forms, including credential stuffing, account takeover, and content scraping. Attackers use bots to automate the brute-force testing of stolen or leaked credentials across multiple websites. This can lead to unauthorized access, fraudulent transactions, and data breaches.

Account takeover attacks involve using compromised credentials to gain unauthorized access to user accounts on various platforms. Once inside, attackers can exploit these accounts for financial gain or engage in malicious activities, such as spreading misinformation.

Content scraping attacks target websites and APIs, where malicious bots scrape valuable content, such as product listings, prices, or user-generated data. This can harm businesses by stealing intellectual property and undermining their competitive advantage.

Another emerging threat is the abuse of Application Programming Interfaces (APIs). APIs enable the interaction between different software systems and are crucial for modern web applications. However, when not properly secured, APIs can become an attractive target for attackers.

API abuse can lead to various security issues, including data breaches, unauthorized access, and denial-of-service attacks. Attackers can exploit API vulnerabilities to extract sensitive information, manipulate data, or disrupt services.

API security involves implementing proper authentication, authorization, rate limiting, and monitoring to mitigate these risks. Organizations must thoroughly assess and secure their APIs to prevent abuse.

Serverless computing has also introduced new security challenges. While serverless platforms offer scalability and cost-effectiveness, they require a different approach to security. Attackers can target serverless functions, exploit misconfigurations, and abuse event triggers.

Security best practices for serverless computing include strong access controls, least privilege principles, code analysis, and runtime monitoring. Organizations need to understand the unique security considerations of serverless architectures and apply appropriate safeguards.

The Internet of Things (IoT) continues to grow, connecting everyday devices to the internet. However, the increasing number of IoT devices brings new security concerns. Weaknesses in device security can lead to privacy violations, data breaches, and remote control by malicious actors.

IoT security requires manufacturers to implement robust security measures, including secure firmware updates, encryption, and authentication. Users must also take steps to protect their IoT devices, such as changing default passwords and updating firmware regularly.

Supply chain attacks have become an emerging threat vector. Attackers target software dependencies and third-party components to inject malicious code or compromise legitimate updates. This can result in widespread compromises and data breaches.

To mitigate supply chain attacks, organizations should adopt a Software Bill of Materials (SBOM) to track and verify software components. Implementing secure update mechanisms and monitoring for suspicious activity in the supply chain can also help defend against these threats.

Machine learning and AI-based attacks pose unique challenges. Attackers can leverage machine learning algorithms to create more convincing phishing emails, bypass security controls, and automate attacks.

Defending against machine learning attacks requires advanced techniques, including the use of AI for threat detection and behavior analysis. Organizations should implement solutions that can adapt and learn from evolving threats.

The growth of edge computing introduces security challenges at the edge of the network. Edge devices, such as routers, gateways, and sensors, can become targets for attacks. Securing edge computing involves strong access controls, device hardening, and regular security updates.

Ransomware attacks continue to evolve, with attackers using more sophisticated techniques and targeting critical infrastructure. The impact of ransomware can be devastating, leading to data loss, operational disruption, and financial losses.

Protecting against ransomware requires a multi-layered defense strategy, including regular data backups, security awareness training, and endpoint protection. Organizations must be prepared to respond effectively if they fall victim to a ransomware attack.

Web application threats will continue to evolve as technology advances. To stay ahead of these emerging threats, organizations must adopt a proactive security posture. This includes ongoing threat intelligence, regular security assessments, and a culture of security awareness.

In summary, the evolving landscape of web application threats presents challenges that require continuous vigilance and adaptation. Sophisticated bot attacks, API abuse, serverless security, IoT vulnerabilities, supply chain attacks, machine learning threats, edge computing risks, and ransomware attacks are among the emerging threats that organizations must address. By staying informed and implementing appropriate security measures, organizations can protect their web applications and data from these evolving threats.

Implementing proactive security best practices is paramount in today's rapidly evolving threat landscape, where cyberattacks are becoming increasingly sophisticated and pervasive. Proactive security measures are designed to anticipate and prevent security incidents before they occur, rather than reacting after an attack has already taken place. Organizations must adopt a proactive security mindset to safeguard their digital assets and data effectively.

One fundamental proactive security practice is to establish a strong and well-defined security policy. This policy should outline the organization's commitment to security, define roles and responsibilities, and set clear expectations for security compliance. A comprehensive security policy serves as a foundation for implementing proactive measures throughout the organization.

Identifying and categorizing assets is a crucial step in proactive security. Organizations should conduct asset inventories to determine the value and importance of their digital resources. This enables prioritization of security efforts and allocation of resources to protect the most critical assets.

Implementing access controls and least privilege principles is essential for proactive security. Access controls restrict who can access specific resources and what actions they can perform. Least privilege ensures that individuals and systems have the minimum level of access necessary to perform their tasks, reducing the attack surface.

Regularly updating and patching software and systems is a proactive security practice that helps prevent known vulnerabilities from being exploited. Organizations should establish patch management processes to ensure timely application of security updates. This mitigates the risk of attacks targeting known weaknesses.

Conducting vulnerability assessments and penetration testing is another proactive security measure. These assessments involve identifying and addressing security vulnerabilities in systems, applications, and networks. Penetration testing simulates real-world attacks to evaluate the organization's readiness and response to threats.

Implementing intrusion detection and prevention systems (IDPS) can help organizations detect and respond to security incidents in real-time. IDPS monitors network traffic and system activity, looking for suspicious patterns or behaviors that may indicate an attack. When unusual activity is detected, the system can trigger automated responses or alert security teams for further investigation.

Effective employee training and security awareness programs are vital components of proactive security. Educated and aware employees are more likely to recognize and report security threats, such as phishing attempts or suspicious emails. Ongoing training ensures that staff members stay informed about evolving threats and best practices.

Implementing strong authentication mechanisms is essential for proactive security. Multi-factor authentication (MFA) adds an extra layer of security by requiring users to provide multiple forms of verification before gaining access. MFA helps prevent unauthorized access even if credentials are compromised.

Encrypting sensitive data at rest and in transit is a proactive security measure that safeguards information from unauthorized access. Encryption converts data into a format that can only be deciphered by authorized parties with the appropriate encryption keys. This is particularly important when handling confidential or personal data.

Proactive security includes the monitoring and analysis of security logs and events. Security information and event management (SIEM) systems can centralize log data and generate alerts for suspicious activities. Regularly reviewing logs helps identify potential security incidents and trends.

Establishing an incident response plan is a proactive security practice that prepares organizations to react swiftly and effectively to security breaches. The plan should define roles and responsibilities, outline response procedures, and include communication strategies for addressing security incidents.

Security audits and assessments, conducted by internal or external teams, help organizations evaluate their security posture and identify areas for improvement. Regularly assessing security controls and practices ensures ongoing proactive security efforts.

Proactive security also involves threat intelligence gathering and analysis. Organizations can benefit from staying informed about emerging threats, vulnerabilities, and attack trends. This knowledge enables them to adjust their security measures proactively.

Security automation and orchestration can enhance proactive security by streamlining repetitive tasks and responses. Automated security tools can quickly identify and mitigate threats, reducing the time and effort required for manual intervention.

Proactive security extends to the supply chain, where organizations should assess and ensure the security of third-party vendors and suppliers. Supplier risk assessments and due diligence help identify potential security risks associated with external partners.

Regularly testing and simulating security incidents, such as tabletop exercises and red teaming, allow organizations to evaluate their incident response and recovery capabilities. These exercises help uncover weaknesses and provide opportunities for improvement.

To maintain proactive security, organizations must stay informed about the evolving threat landscape. This involves monitoring industry trends, participating in security communities, and collaborating with peers to share threat intelligence and best practices.

In summary, proactive security best practices are essential for mitigating security risks and protecting an organization's digital assets and data. These practices encompass establishing security policies, identifying and categorizing assets, implementing access controls, patching software, conducting vulnerability assessments, and deploying intrusion detection systems. Additionally, employee training, strong authentication, encryption, security monitoring, incident response planning, security audits, threat intelligence, and automation play key roles in proactive security efforts. By adopting a proactive security mindset and continually evolving their security measures, organizations can better defend against the ever-changing landscape of cyber threats.

BOOK 3
ADVANCED WEB APPLICATION SECURITY
BEYOND THE OWASP TOP 10

ROB BOTWRIGHT

Chapter 1: Evolving Web Application Threat Landscape

Tracking the shifting landscape of web threats is a continuous and essential task for organizations and security professionals. The threat landscape is dynamic, with new threats emerging, existing threats evolving, and attackers constantly developing new techniques. Understanding these changes is critical to developing effective cybersecurity strategies.

One of the significant shifts in the web threat landscape is the increased sophistication of phishing attacks. Phishing has evolved from basic email scams to highly targeted and convincing campaigns. Attackers use social engineering techniques and personalization to trick users into disclosing sensitive information or downloading malicious content.

Spear phishing is a specific type of phishing attack that targets individuals or organizations with tailored and often highly convincing messages. These attacks can be challenging to detect because they are customized to exploit specific vulnerabilities or leverage personal information.

Another shift in the web threat landscape is the growth of ransomware attacks. Ransomware has become a lucrative business for cybercriminals, leading to the development of ransomware-as-a-service (RaaS) models. Attackers now have access to sophisticated ransomware tools and can target organizations of all sizes.

Ransomware attacks have also evolved to include double extortion tactics, where attackers not only encrypt data but also steal sensitive information, threatening to publish it if a ransom is not paid. This additional leverage puts even more pressure on victims to comply with ransom demands.

Web application attacks remain a persistent threat in the shifting landscape. SQL injection, cross-site scripting (XSS), and remote code execution vulnerabilities continue to be targeted by attackers. Web application attacks can lead to data breaches, unauthorized access, and the compromise of sensitive information.

Distributed Denial of Service (DDoS) attacks have also evolved in complexity and scale. Attackers now employ botnets comprised of thousands or even millions of compromised devices to launch massive DDoS attacks. These attacks can overwhelm even well-protected networks and services.

The adoption of cloud computing has introduced new considerations in the web threat landscape. While cloud providers offer robust security features, organizations are responsible for securing their data and applications in the cloud. Misconfigurations, inadequate access controls, and insecure interfaces can lead to cloud-based breaches.

The Internet of Things (IoT) has brought about a proliferation of connected devices, creating additional attack vectors. Weak security practices in IoT devices can lead to unauthorized access, data breaches, and even device manipulation. Attackers may target IoT devices to create botnets for DDoS attacks or infiltrate home networks.

Supply chain attacks have gained prominence in recent years. Attackers target software vendors and suppliers to inject malicious code or compromise legitimate updates.

This can lead to widespread compromises and data breaches, affecting organizations and their customers.

The threat landscape also includes insider threats, where individuals within an organization pose a risk. Insiders may intentionally or unintentionally disclose sensitive information, manipulate systems, or engage in malicious activities. These threats require a combination of technical controls and security awareness training.

Nation-state actors and advanced persistent threats (APTs) continue to pose significant challenges. These well-funded and highly skilled adversaries target governments, critical infrastructure, and organizations for espionage, data theft, or disruption. Their tactics are sophisticated and persistent, making them challenging to defend against.

The dark web serves as a marketplace for cybercriminals, where they buy and sell tools, services, and stolen data. The anonymity provided by the dark web allows criminals to operate with relative impunity. Monitoring and understanding activities on the dark web are essential for threat intelligence.

Machine learning and artificial intelligence (AI) are being leveraged by both attackers and defenders. Attackers use machine learning algorithms to automate attacks, evade detection, and craft convincing phishing emails. Defenders, in turn, employ AI for threat detection, behavioral analysis, and incident response.

The proliferation of digital currencies, such as Bitcoin, has enabled cybercriminals to receive payments anonymously. Ransomware attackers often demand payments in cryptocurrencies, making it challenging to trace and recover funds. This shift has led to an increase in ransomware attacks.

To track the shifting landscape of web threats effectively, organizations must adopt a comprehensive cybersecurity strategy. This strategy includes continuous threat intelligence gathering, monitoring of emerging trends, vulnerability assessments, and proactive security measures. Collaboration within the cybersecurity community and sharing threat information are also critical components of staying ahead of evolving threats.

Additionally, organizations should invest in cybersecurity training and awareness programs to educate employees about the latest threats and best practices. Regularly updating security policies and incident response plans ensures preparedness for handling various types of threats.

In summary, the web threat landscape is dynamic and constantly evolving. Understanding these shifts is crucial for organizations to adapt their cybersecurity strategies and defenses effectively. Phishing attacks, ransomware, web application vulnerabilities, DDoS attacks, cloud security, IoT risks, supply chain threats, insider threats, nation-state actors, the dark web, AI and machine learning, and cryptocurrency use all contribute to the complexity of the web threat landscape. By staying informed and proactively addressing these challenges, organizations can better protect their digital assets and data in an ever-changing threat environment.

Predicting future web application security challenges is a complex task, as the cybersecurity landscape is constantly evolving, and new threats are continuously emerging.

However, by analyzing current trends and technologies, we can gain insight into potential challenges that may arise in the future. One of the key factors driving future web application security challenges is the increasing complexity of web applications themselves. As organizations develop more feature-rich and interactive web applications, the attack surface for potential vulnerabilities expands.

The adoption of modern web development frameworks and technologies, such as Single Page Applications (SPAs) and Progressive Web Apps (PWAs), introduces new security considerations. These technologies often rely heavily on client-side scripting, which can expose vulnerabilities like Cross-Site Scripting (XSS) and client-side data manipulation. Predicting future web application security challenges involves recognizing the potential impact of emerging technologies.

Another factor to consider is the growing interconnectivity of devices and systems through the Internet of Things (IoT). As more devices become web-enabled and interconnected, the attack surface expands exponentially, creating new opportunities for attackers. IoT devices, often designed with limited security features, can be exploited to gain unauthorized access to networks and data.

Predicting future web application security challenges also requires us to examine the evolving threat landscape. One trend that is likely to continue is the increasing sophistication of cyberattacks. Attackers are becoming more adept at evading traditional security measures and are using advanced techniques to compromise web applications.

Machine learning and artificial intelligence (AI) are expected to play a significant role in future web application security challenges. While these technologies can be used for threat detection and mitigation, they can also be leveraged by attackers to automate attacks and improve their evasion tactics.

The widespread adoption of cloud computing and serverless architectures presents both opportunities and challenges for web application security. While cloud providers offer robust security features, organizations must still ensure that their cloud-based applications and data are adequately protected. Misconfigurations in cloud environments can lead to data breaches and unauthorized access.

Predicting future web application security challenges also involves considering the regulatory landscape. As governments and regulatory bodies become more proactive in enforcing data protection and privacy regulations, organizations will need to ensure compliance with these requirements. Non-compliance can result in legal and financial consequences.

The emergence of quantum computing poses a unique challenge for web application security. Quantum computers have the potential to break widely used encryption algorithms, rendering current cryptographic protections obsolete. Predicting the timeline for quantum computing's impact on web security is uncertain, but organizations should prepare for this eventual challenge.

The growth of application programming interfaces (APIs) also presents security challenges. APIs are essential for connecting different systems and services, but they can introduce vulnerabilities if not properly secured. As the use of APIs continues to expand, organizations must prioritize API security to prevent data breaches and unauthorized access.

Predicting future web application security challenges also requires us to consider the evolving threat landscape from nation-state actors. Nation-states may increasingly target web applications for espionage, data theft, or disruption. Their tactics are likely to become more sophisticated and persistent, making defense against such threats more challenging.

The use of digital currencies, including cryptocurrencies, in cyberattacks is expected to continue to grow. Attackers often demand ransom payments in cryptocurrencies, making it difficult to trace and recover funds. This trend may lead to increased ransomware attacks and financial losses.

The adoption of 5G and edge computing introduces new security considerations. These technologies enable faster data processing and lower latency but also increase the attack surface. Securing edge devices and networks becomes critical in a 5G and edge computing environment.

Predicting future web application security challenges necessitates an emphasis on proactive security measures. Organizations must adopt a proactive security mindset, continuously assess their web applications for vulnerabilities, and prioritize patch management. Security awareness training for employees and security teams is essential to address emerging threats.

Collaboration and information sharing within the cybersecurity community are crucial for staying ahead of evolving challenges. Security professionals should participate in threat intelligence sharing initiatives and remain vigilant for emerging attack patterns and techniques.

In summary, predicting future web application security challenges requires considering multiple factors, including the complexity of web applications, emerging technologies, IoT, evolving threat landscape, machine learning and AI, cloud computing, regulatory compliance, quantum computing, API security, nation-state threats, digital currencies, 5G, and edge computing. Organizations must remain proactive in their approach to security, continually adapt to new threats, and collaborate with the cybersecurity community to defend against evolving challenges.

Chapter 2: Deep Dive into Lesser-Known Vulnerabilities

Exploring the world of web application security reveals a multitude of threats and vulnerabilities that can compromise the integrity, confidentiality, and availability of data. While some vulnerabilities like SQL injection, Cross-Site Scripting (XSS), and Cross-Site Request Forgery (CSRF) are widely recognized and studied, there exist lesser-known vulnerabilities that are equally dangerous but often overlooked. Next, we'll delve into these lesser-known vulnerabilities, shedding light on their characteristics and potential impact.

One such vulnerability is "Server-Side Request Forgery" or SSRF, which occurs when an attacker tricks a web application into making unauthorized requests to internal or external resources. SSRF can lead to data leaks, remote code execution, or the discovery of sensitive information. Understanding how to detect and mitigate SSRF is crucial in securing web applications.

Another lesser-known vulnerability is "XML External Entity (XXE) Injection," where attackers manipulate XML input to exploit vulnerable XML parsers. This can result in data disclosure, server-side request forgery, or even remote code execution. Web developers and security professionals must be aware of XXE and implement proper input validation and protection mechanisms.

The "Server-Side Template Injection" vulnerability is another lesser-known threat that attackers can exploit. This occurs when user input is embedded directly into server-side templates, allowing for remote code execution. Understanding the risks associated with server-side template engines and implementing secure coding practices can prevent this vulnerability.

"CORS (Cross-Origin Resource Sharing) Misconfiguration" is a vulnerability that often goes unnoticed. Improper CORS settings can enable attackers to make unauthorized cross-origin requests, leading to data theft or manipulation. Web developers should configure CORS policies correctly to mitigate this risk.

WebSockets, a technology that enables real-time communication between clients and servers, can introduce security challenges if not properly secured. Attackers may attempt "WebSocket Hijacking" to intercept or manipulate WebSocket traffic. Developers should implement secure WebSocket protocols and encryption to prevent this vulnerability.

Another often underestimated threat is "Deserialization Vulnerabilities," which can lead to remote code execution if not properly addressed. Attackers can exploit flaws in deserialization processes to execute malicious code on the server. Implementing secure deserialization practices and input validation is crucial in preventing these vulnerabilities.

"Clickjacking" is a lesser-known but deceptive attack where attackers trick users into clicking on elements hidden behind legitimate content. Clickjacking can lead to unintended actions or disclosure of sensitive information. Security measures such as frame-busting scripts can help mitigate this threat.

Lesser-known vulnerabilities can also target "File Upload Forms." Attackers may exploit weak validation or insufficient input sanitization to upload malicious files. Implementing strict file upload controls and scanning uploaded files for malware is essential to prevent this type of attack.

The "Security Headers Misconfiguration" vulnerability often escapes attention but can have a significant impact. Failure to set appropriate security headers can expose web applications to various threats, including XSS and clickjacking. Security professionals should ensure that HTTP headers are correctly configured to enhance security.

"Algorithmic Complexity Attacks" can target web applications that rely on inefficient algorithms. Attackers may exploit these inefficiencies to perform denial-of-service attacks. Developers should optimize algorithms and implement rate limiting to protect against such attacks.

Lastly, "Data Validation Bypass" vulnerabilities can occur when web applications do not adequately validate user input. Attackers can manipulate data input to bypass security controls and gain unauthorized access. Proper input validation and enforcing strict data validation rules are essential in preventing this type of vulnerability.

Understanding these lesser-known vulnerabilities is critical for web application security. Security professionals and web developers should stay informed about emerging threats and regularly update their knowledge and security practices. By addressing these vulnerabilities and implementing appropriate safeguards, organizations can better protect their web applications from a wider range of potential threats and attacks.

Mitigation strategies for obscure threats are crucial in maintaining the security of web applications. While many well-known vulnerabilities receive extensive attention and mitigation efforts, obscure threats can often be equally or even more dangerous due to their lesser-known nature. Next, we will explore effective strategies for mitigating these obscure threats and enhancing overall web application security.

Mitigating Server-Side Request Forgery (SSRF) requires validating and sanitizing user inputs to prevent attackers from manipulating requests to access internal resources. Implementing strict input validation and whitelisting external resources can help block unauthorized SSRF attempts. Additionally, limiting the use of sensitive internal resources and employing security controls such as firewalls can further mitigate this threat.

To combat XML External Entity (XXE) Injection, organizations should disable external entity processing and utilize modern parsers that mitigate XXE vulnerabilities. Regularly updating and patching software components that use XML parsing is essential. Implementing proper input validation and sanitization can also help protect against XXE attacks.

Server-Side Template Injection vulnerabilities can be mitigated by implementing secure coding practices and using templates that support context-aware escaping. Web developers should avoid dynamic template rendering when possible and ensure that user inputs are properly validated and sanitized. Implementing Content Security Policy (CSP) headers can also help mitigate the risk associated with server-side template injection.

CORS (Cross-Origin Resource Sharing) misconfigurations can be prevented by correctly configuring CORS policies on web servers. Developers should carefully specify allowed origins, methods, and headers in CORS policies to restrict cross-origin requests. Regularly reviewing and testing CORS configurations can help identify and remediate misconfigurations.

WebSockets should be secured by using the WebSocket Secure (WSS) protocol to encrypt communication. Implementing proper authentication and authorization mechanisms for WebSocket connections is essential. Monitoring WebSocket traffic for suspicious activities and implementing rate limiting can further enhance security.

Mitigating deserialization vulnerabilities involves using secure deserialization libraries, avoiding the use of dangerous deserialization methods, and validating serialized data. Developers should ensure that only trusted data is deserialized and that serialized data is signed or encrypted when transmitted. Implementing strict input validation and monitoring for unusual deserialization activities can also help detect and prevent attacks.

To defend against clickjacking attacks, organizations should implement frame-busting scripts to prevent their web pages from being embedded in malicious frames. Using the X-Frame-Options header with the "DENY" or "SAMEORIGIN" directive can also help protect against clickjacking. Regularly testing web applications for clickjacking vulnerabilities is essential to identify and remediate any potential issues.

Mitigating File Upload Form vulnerabilities requires implementing strict file upload controls and validation. Developers should validate file types, check file content for malware, and use unique filenames to prevent attackers from uploading malicious files. Restricting file uploads to trusted users and implementing access controls on uploaded files can further enhance security.

Security headers misconfigurations can be mitigated by configuring appropriate HTTP security headers, such as Content Security Policy (CSP), Strict-Transport-Security (HSTS), and X-Content-Type-Options. Regularly scanning web applications for security header misconfigurations and performing security headers testing can help identify and remediate issues.

Algorithmic Complexity Attacks can be mitigated by optimizing algorithms and data structures to reduce their computational complexity. Implementing rate limiting and monitoring for unusual patterns of algorithmic complexity can help detect and prevent attacks. Organizations should also regularly review and update their algorithms to address potential vulnerabilities.

Mitigating Data Validation Bypass vulnerabilities requires enforcing strict data validation rules and ensuring that user input is properly validated and sanitized. Developers should implement input validation at multiple levels of the application stack and avoid relying solely on client-side validation. Regularly testing web applications for data validation bypass vulnerabilities is essential to identify and remediate potential weaknesses.

In summary, mitigation strategies for obscure threats are essential components of a robust web application security program. By understanding the characteristics and risks associated with lesser-known vulnerabilities and implementing the appropriate security measures, organizations can enhance their overall security posture. Regular security testing, vulnerability assessments, and continuous monitoring are critical for identifying and addressing obscure threats to web applications. Staying informed about emerging threats and security best practices is also essential for maintaining effective mitigation strategies in a constantly evolving threat landscape.

Chapter 3: Advanced SQL Injection Techniques

Mastering the art of SQL injection attacks is a critical skill for both cybersecurity professionals and malicious hackers. SQL injection is a type of attack that targets the vulnerabilities in an application's database layer, allowing attackers to manipulate the database and potentially gain unauthorized access to sensitive data. Understanding the anatomy of SQL injection attacks is the first step towards mastering this technique.

SQL injection attacks typically occur when an application accepts user input and constructs SQL queries without properly validating or sanitizing that input. The attacker exploits this vulnerability by injecting malicious SQL code into the input fields. The injected code is then executed by the application's database, potentially giving the attacker full control over the database and the ability to extract, modify, or delete data.

One of the most common types of SQL injection attacks is known as "Classic SQL Injection." In a classic SQL injection attack, the attacker inserts malicious SQL statements into input fields, such as login forms or search boxes. If the application does not properly validate or sanitize the input, the malicious SQL code is executed by the database, allowing the attacker to bypass authentication or retrieve sensitive information.

Another variant of SQL injection is "Blind SQL Injection," which is more challenging to detect and exploit. In a blind SQL injection attack, the attacker typically uses Boolean-based or time-based techniques to infer information from the database. This involves sending SQL queries that evaluate to either true or false, and based on the application's response, the attacker deduces whether a condition is met or not.

"Out-of-Band SQL Injection" is a less common but potent form of SQL injection attack. In this scenario, the attacker sends malicious SQL queries that trigger outbound network requests to a server controlled by the attacker. This technique allows the attacker to exfiltrate data from the database through a different channel, making it harder to detect.

Mastering SQL injection attacks involves understanding the various techniques attackers use to craft malicious SQL statements. Attackers often use techniques like UNION-based SQL injection, where they inject a UNION SELECT statement to retrieve data from other database tables. Time-based blind SQL injection is another technique where the attacker induces delays in the application's response to extract information slowly.

The impact of SQL injection attacks can be severe, leading to data breaches, unauthorized access, and financial losses. To master the art of SQL injection attacks, one must also understand the potential consequences and ethical considerations. Cybersecurity professionals must use their knowledge of SQL injection to protect applications and databases from such attacks, rather than exploiting vulnerabilities for malicious purposes.

Preventing SQL injection attacks requires a multi-pronged approach. One fundamental mitigation technique is input validation and sanitization. Web applications should validate and sanitize user input to ensure that it does not contain malicious SQL code. This includes validating input fields, escaping special characters, and using parameterized queries or prepared statements to separate user input from SQL queries.

Web application firewalls (WAFs) can provide an additional layer of defense against SQL injection attacks. WAFs analyze incoming traffic and can block requests that exhibit suspicious SQL injection patterns. Regularly updating and patching software components, including web application frameworks and database systems, is essential to address known vulnerabilities that attackers might exploit.

Security testing and vulnerability assessments are crucial in identifying and mitigating SQL injection vulnerabilities. Regularly scanning web applications for SQL injection vulnerabilities using automated tools and manual testing can help organizations proactively address weaknesses.

To master the art of SQL injection attacks from a defensive perspective, cybersecurity professionals must stay informed about emerging threats and security best practices. They should also understand the principles of secure coding and follow secure development guidelines to prevent SQL injection vulnerabilities from being introduced in the first place.

Mastering the art of SQL injection attacks can be a double-edged sword. While understanding the techniques and consequences of SQL injection is essential for cybersecurity professionals to defend against such attacks, it is equally important to use this knowledge ethically and responsibly. Ultimately, the goal should be to protect applications and data from SQL injection vulnerabilities and help secure the digital landscape for all users.

Advanced defenses against SQL injection attacks are

essential in protecting web applications and databases from increasingly sophisticated threats. While basic security measures like input validation and parameterized queries provide a foundation for SQL injection prevention, advanced techniques and strategies are required to stay ahead of determined attackers. Next, we will explore advanced defenses that can significantly enhance the security of your applications.

One advanced defense strategy is the use of Web Application Firewalls (WAFs) equipped with SQL injection detection and prevention capabilities. WAFs analyze incoming web traffic in real-time and can detect and block SQL injection attempts based on predefined rules and patterns. They provide an additional layer of security that can help mitigate attacks before they reach the application server.

Implementing a robust Content Security Policy (CSP) is another advanced defense technique. CSP is a security feature that enables web developers to specify which resources can be loaded and executed on a web page. By implementing a strict CSP, you can mitigate the risk of XSS attacks, which are often used in conjunction with SQL injection attacks to deliver malicious payloads.

Query parameterization, often referred to as "prepared statements," is an advanced defense technique that separates SQL code from user input entirely. In a prepared statement, placeholders are used in SQL queries, and user input is bound to these placeholders. This approach ensures that user input is never directly incorporated into the SQL query, making SQL injection attacks virtually impossible.

Database firewalls are specialized security solutions designed to protect databases from various threats, including SQL injection. They monitor database traffic, analyze SQL queries, and can block or log suspicious queries in real-time. Implementing a database firewall as part of your security infrastructure can add an extra layer of defense against SQL injection attacks.

The principle of "Least Privilege" is a fundamental security concept that plays a crucial role in advanced SQL injection defenses. Database users and application accounts should be granted the minimum privileges necessary to perform their tasks. By limiting the permissions associated with each user or account, you reduce the potential impact of a successful SQL injection attack.

Advanced defenses against SQL injection also involve extensive input validation and sanitization. Regular expressions and pattern matching can be used to validate user input for specific formats, such as email addresses or phone numbers. Additionally, input data should be sanitized to remove or escape any special characters that could be used in SQL injection attacks.

Monitoring and auditing database activities are essential aspects of advanced SQL injection defenses. Real-time monitoring of database queries and activities can help identify abnormal or suspicious behavior. Auditing capabilities can track and log changes made to the database, enabling forensic analysis and incident response.

Implementing rate limiting and request throttling can be effective in defending against SQL injection attacks. These measures restrict the number of queries or requests that can be made within a specified time frame. By limiting the rate at which requests can be made, attackers are hindered in their attempts to launch large-scale SQL injection attacks.

Advanced SQL injection defenses should also include regular security testing and vulnerability assessments. Penetration testing, code reviews, and automated scanning tools can help identify vulnerabilities that may be exploited by attackers. By proactively addressing these weaknesses, organizations can reduce the risk of SQL injection attacks.

Web developers and security professionals should stay informed about emerging SQL injection techniques and tactics. Attackers are constantly evolving their methods, so defenders must continuously update their knowledge and adapt their defenses accordingly. Participating in security communities, attending conferences, and staying updated on security blogs and publications are essential for staying ahead of the curve.

Intrusion detection and prevention systems (IDPS) can complement advanced SQL injection defenses. IDPS solutions monitor network traffic and can detect and block suspicious activities, including SQL injection attempts. When integrated with other security measures, IDPS can provide an additional layer of protection.

Threat intelligence sharing and collaboration with other organizations can enhance advanced SQL injection defenses. Sharing information about known threats and attack patterns can help the security community collectively defend against SQL injection attacks. Collaboration can also lead to the development of shared threat indicators and improved detection mechanisms.

In summary, advanced defenses against SQL injection attacks are crucial for protecting web applications and databases from evolving threats. By implementing a combination of advanced techniques, including Web Application Firewalls, Content Security Policies, query parameterization, database firewalls, the principle of Least Privilege, input validation, monitoring, rate limiting, security testing, and threat intelligence sharing, organizations can significantly reduce the risk of SQL injection attacks. Staying proactive, vigilant, and informed is key to maintaining effective defenses in an ever-changing cybersecurity landscape.

Chapter 4: Multi-Factor Authentication and Secure Session Management

Strengthening security with multi-factor authentication (MFA) is a critical step in safeguarding sensitive data and accounts in today's digital world. MFA, also known as two-factor authentication (2FA) or two-step verification, adds an extra layer of protection beyond traditional username and password combinations. Next, we will explore the importance of MFA, its various forms, and how organizations and individuals can implement it to enhance security.

The reliance on usernames and passwords alone is no longer sufficient to protect against the ever-increasing threats posed by cybercriminals. Weak or stolen passwords are a common attack vector, and the consequences of a security breach can be devastating. MFA addresses these vulnerabilities by requiring users to provide multiple forms of verification before granting access.

One of the most common forms of MFA is something you know and something you have. This typically involves a combination of a password or PIN (something you know) and a physical device or token (something you have), such as a smartphone or hardware security key. When a user attempts to log in, they must provide both factors to prove their identity.

Biometric authentication, such as fingerprint or facial recognition, is another form of MFA that relies on something you are. Biometrics add an additional layer of security by verifying a user's unique physiological or behavioral characteristics. However, it's important to note that biometric data should be stored and handled securely to prevent misuse.

Time-based one-time passwords (TOTP) are commonly used in MFA implementations. With TOTP, a user receives a temporary code on their registered device, which must be entered within a specific timeframe to gain access. This adds a time-sensitive element to the authentication process, enhancing security.

MFA can also be based on something you do, such as a specific action or gesture. For example, a user might need to perform a particular gesture on a touchscreen device or click a specific area on an image to complete the authentication process. These dynamic actions add an additional layer of complexity for attackers to overcome.

Organizations can implement MFA for various systems and applications, including email accounts, online banking, cloud services, and more. By requiring users to authenticate with multiple factors, organizations significantly reduce the risk of unauthorized access and data breaches.

Implementing MFA often involves the use of authentication apps or security tokens. Authentication apps generate one-time codes that users must enter during the login process. Security tokens, on the other hand, are physical devices that generate time-based or event-based codes. Both methods enhance security by adding an extra layer of verification.

Many online services and platforms offer MFA as an option for users to enable. Users can typically choose the MFA method that best suits their preferences and needs. Common MFA methods include sending codes via SMS, using mobile apps like Google Authenticator or Authy, and employing hardware tokens like YubiKey.

One of the critical benefits of MFA is its effectiveness in preventing unauthorized access even if an attacker obtains the user's password. Without the additional factor, such as a time-sensitive code or a biometric scan, the attacker cannot complete the authentication process. This significantly raises the bar for cybercriminals trying to compromise accounts.

While MFA greatly enhances security, it is not without challenges. Users may find the initial setup and additional steps during login somewhat inconvenient. Balancing security and user experience is essential, and organizations should provide clear instructions and support for MFA adoption.

Phishing attacks remain a concern even with MFA in place. Attackers may attempt to trick users into providing their multi-factor authentication codes or compromise their authentication apps. Education and awareness campaigns are essential to help users recognize phishing attempts and protect their MFA credentials.

Organizations should also implement additional security measures, such as account lockout policies and monitoring for unusual login activity, to further enhance security in conjunction with MFA.

For individuals, enabling MFA on their accounts is a straightforward yet impactful step towards securing their online presence. Many popular online services and platforms offer MFA options in their account settings. Users should take advantage of these features to protect their data and privacy.

In summary, strengthening security with multi-factor authentication is a vital strategy in today's digital landscape. MFA provides an effective defense against password-related vulnerabilities and significantly reduces the risk of unauthorized access and data breaches. Both organizations and individuals should embrace MFA as an essential tool in their cybersecurity arsenal to safeguard their valuable information and assets.

Secure session management is a fundamental aspect of web application security, and it goes beyond the basics of simply creating and maintaining user sessions. Next, we will explore advanced concepts and techniques for securing user sessions in web applications. Effective session management is crucial because it determines how user data and access are maintained during a user's interaction with an application. Session management involves the creation, tracking, and termination of user sessions, which are essential for maintaining the state and user context across multiple HTTP requests.

Session management becomes more complex in modern web applications where users can access an application from various devices and locations. For instance, a user might log in from a desktop computer at home, switch to a smartphone while commuting, and then continue their session on a tablet at work. To ensure the security and continuity of user sessions in such scenarios, web developers must adopt advanced session management strategies.

One of the fundamental principles of secure session management is session identifier generation. Session identifiers, also known as session tokens, are unique pieces of data that link a user to their session on the server. It's essential to generate secure and unpredictable session identifiers to prevent session fixation attacks, where an attacker sets a user's session ID to a known value.

To generate secure session identifiers, cryptographic random number generators (CSPRNGs) should be used. These generators produce unpredictable and unique values that are resistant to guessing or brute force attacks. Developers should avoid using predictable identifiers, such as sequential numbers or timestamps, as they can be easily guessed by attackers.

Session timeouts are another critical aspect of secure session management. Timeouts define how long a user's session remains active after their last interaction with the application. Implementing appropriate session timeouts is essential to prevent session hijacking in cases where a user leaves their session unattended or forgets to log out.

For example, if a user leaves their computer unattended and an attacker gains physical access, a long session timeout could allow the attacker to take control of the user's session. To mitigate this risk, session timeouts should be set to reasonably short intervals, forcing users to reauthenticate if they are idle for an extended period.

Session fixation attacks can occur when an attacker tricks a user into adopting a session ID controlled by the attacker. To defend against session fixation, web applications should generate a new session identifier for each user upon login. The old session identifier should be invalidated to ensure that it cannot be used by the attacker.

Implementing secure logout mechanisms is essential for proper session management. When a user logs out, their session on the server should be immediately terminated. Additionally, all session-related data, such as session cookies or tokens stored on the client side, should be invalidated and removed. Failure to do so may allow an attacker to continue using a session even after the user has logged out.

Session storage mechanisms play a crucial role in secure session management. Session data can be stored on the server-side, client-side, or a combination of both. Server-side storage is generally more secure as it reduces the risk of client-side attacks, such as session theft or tampering. However, server-side storage can impact scalability and performance, especially in distributed or cloud-based applications.

When using client-side storage for session data, it's important to encrypt and sign the data to prevent unauthorized access or tampering. Modern web frameworks often provide tools and libraries to handle secure session storage and management. Web developers should leverage these resources to ensure the integrity and confidentiality of session data.

Cross-Site Scripting (XSS) attacks pose a significant threat to session management. An attacker who successfully injects malicious scripts into a web application can steal session cookies or manipulate session data. To defend against XSS attacks, web developers should implement proper input validation, output encoding, and secure cookie settings.

HttpOnly and Secure flags on session cookies are essential security measures. The HttpOnly flag prevents JavaScript from accessing the session cookie, reducing the risk of XSS attacks. The Secure flag ensures that the cookie is transmitted only over secure (HTTPS) connections, protecting it from interception by attackers on unsecured networks.

Cross-Site Request Forgery (CSRF) attacks are another challenge for session management. In CSRF attacks, attackers trick users into performing actions without their knowledge or consent while using their authenticated session. To defend against CSRF attacks, web applications should implement anti-CSRF tokens and validate incoming requests to ensure they match the expected state.

Session revocation is an advanced technique for secure session management. It allows users to revoke their sessions remotely, such as logging out from another device or location. Implementing session revocation requires a robust backend infrastructure to manage and coordinate session termination across different application instances.

User-friendly session management is also a consideration in modern web applications. Users should have the ability to view and manage their active sessions. This feature empowers users to monitor and terminate sessions if they suspect unauthorized access or unusual activity.

In summary, secure session management is a multifaceted aspect of web application security that goes beyond the basics. Web developers must consider various factors, including session identifier generation, session timeouts, session fixation, secure logout, storage mechanisms, defense against XSS and CSRF attacks, cookie settings, and even user-friendly features like session viewing and revocation. By implementing advanced session management techniques, web applications can maintain a high level of security and protect user data and privacy in an ever-evolving threat landscape.

Chapter 5: Advanced Cross-Site Scripting (XSS) Defense

Advanced XSS (Cross-Site Scripting) attack vectors represent a significant challenge in web application security, as attackers continuously develop new techniques to exploit vulnerabilities and compromise user data. Next, we will delve into the world of advanced XSS attack vectors, exploring their intricacies and discussing effective countermeasures. XSS attacks occur when an attacker injects malicious scripts into a web application, which are then executed in the context of a user's browser. One advanced XSS attack vector is DOM-based XSS, which involves manipulating the Document Object Model (DOM) of a web page. In DOM-based XSS attacks, the malicious script modifies the page's structure or content after it has been loaded, leading to unpredictable and potentially harmful consequences. Countermeasures for DOM-based XSS include input validation and output encoding, as well as careful design of JavaScript functions and event handlers. Another advanced XSS variant is stored XSS, where the injected script is permanently stored on the web application's server and served to users who access a specific page or resource. Stored XSS attacks can have a lasting impact, as the malicious script continues to execute whenever users load the compromised page. To defend against stored XSS, web developers must implement rigorous input validation, output encoding, and secure storage practices for user-generated content.

Blind XSS attacks present a unique challenge, as the attacker does not directly observe the effects of the exploit. In blind XSS, the malicious payload sends data to a remote server controlled by the attacker, making it difficult to detect and analyze the attack. Web application security teams should conduct thorough penetration testing and security assessments to uncover blind XSS vulnerabilities and assess their potential impact.

Reflective XSS attacks involve the immediate execution of the injected script, typically through a manipulated URL or input field. These attacks rely on tricking users into clicking on a malicious link or visiting a compromised web page. Countermeasures for reflective XSS include input validation, output encoding, and the use of Content Security Policy (CSP) to restrict the sources of executable scripts.

XSS attacks can be used to steal user credentials, session cookies, and sensitive information. Session hijacking is a common goal of attackers who exploit XSS vulnerabilities. Web developers must ensure that sensitive data is never exposed in client-side scripts and that proper session management practices are in place to prevent session theft.

A particularly dangerous advanced XSS attack vector is keylogging, where an attacker captures a user's keystrokes and sends them to a remote server. Keyloggers can record passwords, credit card numbers, and other confidential information. Defending against keyloggers requires the use of secure input fields and the implementation of client-side security mechanisms to detect and block suspicious script activity.

The use of JavaScript obfuscation techniques is prevalent among attackers to evade detection and make malicious scripts more challenging to analyze. Obfuscation involves modifying the script's code to make it appear benign or to bypass security filters. Web application security tools and scanners should be capable of identifying and deobfuscating obfuscated scripts.

Effective countermeasures against advanced XSS attack vectors include the use of Web Application Firewalls (WAFs) equipped with XSS detection and prevention capabilities. WAFs can analyze incoming web traffic in real-time and block malicious scripts based on predefined rules and patterns. Regularly updating WAF rules is essential to stay protected against evolving attack techniques.

Content Security Policy (CSP) is a valuable defense mechanism for mitigating the impact of XSS attacks. CSP allows web developers to specify which sources of content are trusted and can be executed on a web page. By implementing a strict CSP policy, organizations can reduce the risk of XSS attacks by limiting the sources from which scripts can be loaded.

Web developers should also adopt secure coding practices and libraries that help prevent XSS vulnerabilities. Frameworks and libraries like React, Angular, and Vue.js incorporate security features to mitigate XSS risks. By using such tools and following secure coding guidelines, developers can minimize the potential for introducing XSS vulnerabilities in their code.

Security headers, such as the X-XSS-Protection header, should be used to instruct browsers to enable their built-in XSS filters. While these filters are not foolproof, they provide an additional layer of defense against certain XSS attacks. Web administrators should configure security headers appropriately to enhance protection.

Regular security testing, including code reviews and penetration testing, is essential for identifying and addressing XSS vulnerabilities. Automated scanning tools can help discover and remediate XSS issues in web applications. However, manual testing and code review by experienced security professionals are crucial for uncovering complex and advanced XSS attack vectors.

In summary, advanced XSS attack vectors pose a significant threat to web applications and user data. Defending against these attacks requires a combination of robust countermeasures, including input validation, output encoding, secure storage, Web Application Firewalls, Content Security Policy (CSP), secure coding practices, security headers, and thorough security testing. By adopting a multi-layered approach to XSS prevention and staying vigilant against evolving attack techniques, organizations can reduce the risk of XSS vulnerabilities and protect their users from harm. Building robust protection against XSS (Cross-Site Scripting) attacks is paramount in ensuring the security of web applications and safeguarding user data. Next, we will explore strategies and best practices to create a strong defense against XSS vulnerabilities, both in development and post-deployment phases. Effective protection against XSS attacks begins with proper input validation and sanitation. Web developers should validate all incoming data, including user inputs and parameters, to ensure they conform to expected patterns and types. This helps to filter out potentially malicious data and reduces the likelihood of attackers injecting scripts.

In addition to validation, input data should be sanitized before being displayed in web pages. Sanitization involves removing or escaping potentially dangerous characters or code from user inputs. By sanitizing data, web developers can prevent malicious scripts from being executed when the content is rendered in the browser.

Encoding output data is another critical defense mechanism against XSS attacks. Output encoding ensures that any user-generated or dynamic content displayed on a web page is treated as plain text and not executable code. This approach effectively neutralizes any injected scripts, rendering them harmless.

To simplify the implementation of input validation, sanitation, and output encoding, web developers should leverage security libraries and frameworks designed to handle these tasks securely. Many modern web development frameworks provide built-in features and functions for secure data handling, reducing the risk of introducing XSS vulnerabilities through custom code.

Content Security Policy (CSP) is a powerful defense mechanism against XSS attacks. CSP allows web developers to specify which sources of content are trusted and can be executed on a web page. By configuring CSP, organizations can effectively control the types of scripts that can be loaded and executed, reducing the attack surface for XSS vulnerabilities.

Implementing a strong CSP policy requires careful consideration of the application's functionality and the sources of external content it relies on. Web developers must strike a balance between allowing necessary scripts and blocking potentially harmful ones. Regularly monitoring and adjusting the CSP policy based on application behavior and security needs is essential for maintaining protection against evolving threats.

Insecure Direct Object References (IDOR) can be exploited by attackers to manipulate URLs and gain unauthorized access to sensitive resources. To defend against IDOR attacks, web applications should employ proper access controls and session management. Sensitive resources should only be accessible to authorized users with appropriate privileges.

Using Anti-CSRF (Cross-Site Request Forgery) tokens is an effective countermeasure against CSRF attacks that often accompany XSS attacks. Anti-CSRF tokens are unique values generated for each user session and associated with specific actions. These tokens must be included in requests to ensure that the user is intentionally performing the action.

Web application security scanners and vulnerability assessment tools play a crucial role in identifying and remediating XSS vulnerabilities. Organizations should conduct regular security testing to proactively discover and address any potential weaknesses. Automated scanners can help uncover XSS vulnerabilities in web applications and assist in the remediation process.

Code reviews and static analysis of source code are essential components of a comprehensive security strategy. Developers and security experts should review code for potential XSS vulnerabilities, examining input validation, output encoding, and proper handling of user-generated content. Static code analysis tools can also aid in identifying security issues within the source code.

Security awareness and training are vital for both developers and end-users. Developers should receive training on secure coding practices, understanding the risks associated with XSS attacks, and the importance of implementing security measures. End-users should be educated about the potential dangers of executing scripts from untrusted sources and encouraged to exercise caution when interacting with web content.

Web application firewalls (WAFs) equipped with XSS detection and prevention capabilities can provide an additional layer of protection. WAFs analyze incoming web traffic in real-time and block malicious scripts based on predefined rules and patterns. Regularly updating WAF rules is essential to stay protected against evolving attack techniques. Incident response plans should be in place to address potential XSS attacks promptly. When an attack is detected, organizations should have procedures in place to investigate, mitigate, and recover from the incident. This includes identifying the root cause, implementing necessary fixes, and notifying affected parties if sensitive data is compromised. In summary, building robust protection against XSS attacks requires a multi-faceted approach that combines input validation, sanitation, output encoding, the use of security libraries and frameworks, Content Security Policy (CSP), access controls, Anti-CSRF tokens, security testing, code reviews, security awareness, and the use of Web Application Firewalls (WAFs). By implementing these strategies and best practices throughout the development lifecycle and beyond, organizations can significantly reduce the risk of XSS vulnerabilities and enhance the security of their web applications, protecting both their data and their users from harm.

Chapter 6: Protecting Against Access Control Bypass Attacks

Incorporating security into the development lifecycle is essential to building robust and secure web applications. To achieve this, organizations must adopt a proactive approach that considers security at every stage of the development process. This chapter explores the strategies and best practices for seamlessly integrating security into the development lifecycle.

The first step in incorporating security into the development lifecycle is to establish a security culture within the organization. This involves promoting awareness of security risks and the importance of secure coding practices among developers, testers, and other stakeholders. Creating a security-conscious mindset helps ensure that security is a priority from the outset.

Security requirements should be defined and documented early in the development process. These requirements should align with industry standards, best practices, and the specific security needs of the application. By clearly articulating security expectations, developers have a clear roadmap for building secure features.

Threat modeling is a valuable practice that helps identify potential security risks and vulnerabilities early in the development lifecycle. Through threat modeling, teams can systematically analyze the application's architecture, data flow, and potential attack vectors to identify areas that require special attention. This proactive approach allows developers to address security concerns before they become significant issues.

Secure coding guidelines and best practices should be established and followed throughout the development process. Developers should be well-versed in secure coding principles, such as input validation, output encoding, and avoiding common security pitfalls like SQL injection and XSS. Code reviews and static analysis tools can help ensure that code adheres to these guidelines.

Integrating security testing into the development pipeline is crucial for identifying and mitigating vulnerabilities. Automated security testing tools can scan code and configurations for known vulnerabilities, providing developers with feedback on potential issues. Regular dynamic application security testing (DAST) and static application security testing (SAST) help catch vulnerabilities early.

Continuous integration and continuous deployment (CI/CD) pipelines should include security checks as part of the build and deployment process. Automated security testing, vulnerability scanning, and code analysis should be integrated into CI/CD workflows to catch security issues before they reach production. This ensures that secure code is deployed consistently.

Security champions or dedicated security personnel should be part of the development team. These individuals have expertise in security and can guide developers, provide training, and conduct security reviews throughout the development process. Having security expertise readily available helps address security concerns effectively.

Regular security training and awareness programs should be conducted for all team members. Developers, testers, and other stakeholders should be educated about the latest security threats, vulnerabilities, and best practices. Security training helps ensure that everyone on the team is well-informed and can contribute to a secure development process.

Security assessments and penetration testing should be conducted on the application before it is deployed. These assessments simulate real-world attacks to identify vulnerabilities that may have been missed during development. By identifying and addressing vulnerabilities in the testing phase, organizations can reduce the risk of security incidents in production.

Security incident response plans should be developed and tested in advance. In the event of a security breach or incident, having a well-defined plan in place ensures that the team can respond quickly and effectively. This includes containing the incident, investigating the root cause, and implementing remediation measures.

Regular security reviews and audits should be conducted to assess the application's security posture. These reviews help organizations identify areas that may have been overlooked and ensure that security controls are functioning as intended. Security audits provide valuable insights into the application's overall security.

Ongoing monitoring and maintenance are critical to maintaining the security of web applications. Security patches and updates should be applied promptly to address known vulnerabilities. Additionally, monitoring for suspicious activity and unauthorized access can help detect security incidents in real-time.

Security documentation should be comprehensive and readily available to all team members. This includes documentation of security requirements, threat models, secure coding guidelines, and incident response plans. Having accessible documentation ensures that everyone on the team can reference and follow security practices.

In summary, incorporating security into the development lifecycle requires a holistic approach that considers security from the beginning to the end of the development process. Establishing a security culture, defining security requirements, conducting threat modeling, following secure coding practices, integrating security testing, and having security champions are essential elements. Regular security training, assessments, incident response planning, reviews, and ongoing monitoring and maintenance further strengthen the security posture. By following these strategies and best practices, organizations can build and maintain secure web applications that protect both their data and their users from potential threats.

Chapter 7: Security by Design: Building Resilient Applications

Designing resilient applications that are inherently secure is paramount in today's digital landscape, where cyber threats are constantly evolving. To achieve this, developers and architects must adhere to secure design principles that fortify applications against potential vulnerabilities and attacks. Next, we will explore these principles and how they can be applied to create robust and secure web applications.

The principle of defense in depth emphasizes the importance of layering security controls throughout an application's architecture. By implementing multiple layers of security, such as firewalls, access controls, and encryption, an application becomes more resilient to attacks. This approach ensures that if one security measure is breached, others provide additional protection.

Secure by default is a fundamental principle that encourages developers to configure applications with security in mind from the outset. This means that applications should be designed to be secure even if no additional security measures are applied. By default, access to sensitive data or functionality should be restricted, and only authorized users or processes should have access.

Least privilege is a principle that restricts users, processes, or systems to the minimum level of access required to perform their tasks. By adhering to the principle of least privilege, developers reduce the attack surface and limit the potential impact of security breaches. This principle ensures that individuals or systems only have access to what is necessary for their role or function.

The principle of fail securely focuses on ensuring that when an application encounters an error or failure, it does so in a way that does not compromise security. This means that error messages should not reveal sensitive information, and the application should gracefully handle failures without exposing vulnerabilities.

Input validation is a critical secure design principle that involves validating and sanitizing all user inputs to prevent malicious input from reaching the application's core logic. By thoroughly validating and sanitizing inputs, developers can prevent common vulnerabilities such as SQL injection and cross-site scripting (XSS) attacks. Input validation should be applied at all entry points where user data is accepted.

Output encoding is a complementary principle that involves encoding output data to prevent potential injection attacks, such as XSS. Developers should ensure that user-generated content, such as input fields and user-generated text, is properly encoded before rendering it in a web page. Output encoding helps protect against attacks that attempt to inject malicious scripts into the application's output.

Secure communication is a principle that focuses on encrypting data in transit to protect it from eavesdropping and interception. Developers should use secure communication protocols, such as HTTPS, to ensure that data transmitted between the client and server is encrypted. This principle helps safeguard sensitive data, such as login credentials and personal information.

Authentication and authorization are essential secure design principles that ensure that users are who they claim to be and that they have the appropriate permissions to access specific resources or functionality. Strong authentication mechanisms, such as multi-factor authentication (MFA), should be implemented to verify user identities. Authorization controls should restrict access based on user roles and permissions.

Session management is a critical principle that involves securely managing user sessions to prevent session fixation, session hijacking, and other session-related attacks. Developers should use secure session management techniques, such as generating unique session identifiers and implementing session timeouts. Secure session management helps protect user sessions from unauthorized access. Error handling and logging are principles that focus on how applications handle errors and log events. Developers should ensure that error messages do not reveal sensitive information and that logs are generated and monitored for security-related events. Effective error handling and logging can help identify and respond to security incidents.

Secure storage is a principle that emphasizes the secure storage of sensitive data, such as passwords and encryption keys. Developers should use strong encryption algorithms and key management practices to protect data at rest. Secure storage safeguards sensitive information from unauthorized access or theft.

Security patches and updates are crucial principles that require applications to be regularly updated with security patches and fixes. Developers should stay informed about security vulnerabilities in third-party libraries and components used in their applications. Promptly applying security patches helps mitigate known vulnerabilities.

Security testing and code reviews are principles that involve conducting security assessments and reviews of the application's code and configurations. Regular security testing, including dynamic application security testing (DAST) and static application security testing (SAST), can help identify vulnerabilities. Code reviews by security experts can also uncover security issues and provide recommendations for improvements.

Documentation is a principle that emphasizes the importance of documenting security-related aspects of the application. This includes security requirements, threat models, secure coding guidelines, and incident response plans. Documentation ensures that all team members are aware of security practices and can reference them when needed.

In summary, secure design principles play a crucial role in creating resilient and secure web applications. These principles, including defense in depth, secure by default, least privilege, fail securely, input validation, output encoding, secure communication, authentication and authorization, session management, error handling and logging, secure storage, security patches and updates, security testing and code reviews, and documentation, guide developers and architects in building applications that are inherently secure. By incorporating these principles into the design and development process, organizations can minimize security risks and protect their applications and users from potential threats and vulnerabilities.

Chapter 8: Advanced Cross-Site Request Forgery (CSRF) Protection

In the realm of web application security, understanding advanced CSRF attack scenarios is crucial for building robust defenses. Developers and security professionals must be prepared to counteract increasingly sophisticated attacks. Next, we will explore some of these advanced CSRF attack scenarios and the countermeasures that can be employed to mitigate them.

One advanced CSRF attack scenario involves leveraging malicious JavaScript code to trigger unauthorized actions on a user's behalf. In this scenario, an attacker may embed a hidden iframe or image tag within a malicious website. When a victim visits the attacker's site while authenticated to a target application, the embedded JavaScript code automatically sends requests to the target application, potentially performing actions without the user's consent.

Countermeasures against this type of attack include implementing the SameSite attribute for cookies and using anti-CSRF tokens. The SameSite attribute restricts cookies to only be sent in same-site requests, reducing the risk of cross-site request forgery. Anti-CSRF tokens, also known as synchronizer tokens, are unique tokens generated for each user session and included in forms. The application verifies the token with each request, ensuring that it originates from a legitimate source.

Another advanced CSRF attack scenario involves exploiting Cross-Origin Resource Sharing (CORS) misconfigurations. CORS is a security feature that controls which domains can make requests to a web application. If an application's CORS policy is misconfigured, it may allow requests from unauthorized domains, enabling attackers to perform CSRF attacks across different origins.

Countermeasures for CORS-related CSRF attacks include configuring CORS policies correctly and implementing the previously mentioned anti-CSRF tokens. By configuring CORS policies to allow only trusted domains to access the application's resources, developers can prevent unauthorized cross-origin requests. Additionally, anti-CSRF tokens remain effective in mitigating CSRF attacks, even when CORS policies are misconfigured.

Sophisticated attackers may also attempt to exploit vulnerabilities in third-party plugins or components used by an application. For example, if an application relies on a vulnerable library, an attacker can craft CSRF attacks specifically targeting those vulnerabilities.

To defend against this scenario, it is essential to keep all third-party components and libraries up to date. Developers should regularly monitor security advisories for the components they use and apply patches or updates promptly. Performing security assessments on third-party code and libraries can help identify vulnerabilities and assess the overall security of the application.

One of the more intricate CSRF attack scenarios involves chained attacks that combine multiple vulnerabilities to achieve a specific outcome. For instance, an attacker may start by exploiting a weak password reset mechanism to compromise a user's account. They can then use the compromised account to perform actions within the application, such as transferring funds or changing account settings, all without the user's knowledge or consent.

Countermeasures for chained CSRF attacks include strong authentication and authorization controls, along with comprehensive security testing. Implementing multi-factor authentication (MFA) can significantly enhance account security, making it more challenging for attackers to compromise accounts. Additionally, comprehensive security testing, including penetration testing and vulnerability assessments, can help identify and remediate vulnerabilities before attackers can exploit them in chained attacks.

Cross-Site Request Forgery attacks can become even more challenging to detect when combined with other attack techniques. For example, an attacker may use a CSRF attack in conjunction with a blind Cross-Site Scripting (XSS) vulnerability. The XSS vulnerability allows the attacker to inject malicious JavaScript into a victim's browser, while the CSRF attack forces the victim to take actions within the application.

To mitigate this advanced scenario, organizations should prioritize secure coding practices and security testing. Secure coding practices, such as input validation and output encoding, can help prevent XSS vulnerabilities. Regular security testing, including both dynamic and static analysis, can help identify and address vulnerabilities that attackers might combine in complex attacks.

In some instances, attackers may attempt to exploit CSRF vulnerabilities in combination with other attack vectors to bypass security controls. For example, an attacker might use CSRF to manipulate the settings of an application and then use other vulnerabilities, such as Cross-Site Scripting

(XSS) or SQL injection, to further compromise the application's security.

Countermeasures for these complex attack scenarios include implementing robust security controls at multiple layers. Developers should ensure that input validation and output encoding are applied consistently to prevent XSS and SQL injection vulnerabilities. Network-level security controls, such as Web Application Firewalls (WAFs), can also help detect and block suspicious traffic associated with CSRF attacks.

In summary, advanced CSRF attack scenarios require organizations to adopt a multifaceted approach to security. Countermeasures, such as SameSite attributes, anti-CSRF tokens, correct CORS configuration, strong authentication, patch management, security testing, and secure coding practices, are essential in mitigating CSRF attacks. By understanding and addressing these advanced scenarios, organizations can enhance their web application security and protect against increasingly sophisticated threats.

Protecting against Cross-Site Request Forgery (CSRF) attacks is a critical aspect of web application security. To ensure comprehensive CSRF protection, it's essential to adopt a combination of strategies and best practices. Next, we will explore these comprehensive CSRF protection strategies and how they can be effectively implemented.

First and foremost, it is crucial to understand the fundamentals of CSRF attacks to design effective defenses. A CSRF attack occurs when an attacker tricks a user into executing unintended actions on a web application without their knowledge or consent. These actions can range from changing account settings to initiating financial transactions.

One key strategy for comprehensive CSRF protection is the use of anti-CSRF tokens. Anti-CSRF tokens are unique, random values generated for each user session and associated with specific actions or requests. These tokens are included in forms, links, or AJAX requests and must be submitted along with the request. The application validates the token to ensure that the request is legitimate.

Implementing anti-CSRF tokens helps ensure that only authenticated users can perform actions within the application. Even if an attacker manages to trick a user into executing a CSRF attack, they won't have access to the anti-CSRF token, making the attack ineffective.

Furthermore, anti-CSRF tokens should be securely generated and stored. They should have a sufficient degree of randomness to prevent attackers from predicting or guessing them. Using cryptographic libraries to generate these tokens can enhance their security.

Another important aspect of comprehensive CSRF protection is enforcing the SameSite attribute for cookies. The SameSite attribute restricts the scope of cookies, ensuring they are only sent with same-site requests. This means that cookies won't be included in cross-origin requests, mitigating the risk of CSRF attacks.

By setting the SameSite attribute to "Strict" or "Lax," developers can significantly reduce the potential for CSRF vulnerabilities. For example, setting it to "Strict" ensures that cookies are not sent with cross-origin requests at all, while "Lax" allows cookies to be sent with top-level navigations initiated by a user, but not with subresource requests.

Additionally, secure authentication practices play a critical role in CSRF protection. Implementing strong authentication mechanisms, such as multi-factor authentication (MFA), can significantly enhance security. MFA requires users to provide multiple forms of authentication, making it much harder for attackers to impersonate them.

Furthermore, developers should prioritize secure session management to prevent session fixation and session hijacking, which can be used in conjunction with CSRF attacks. Session management techniques, such as generating unique session identifiers and implementing session timeouts, help safeguard user sessions from unauthorized access.

Another valuable strategy is configuring Cross-Origin Resource Sharing (CORS) policies correctly. CORS policies define which domains are allowed to make requests to a web application. By configuring these policies to only allow trusted domains to access resources, developers can prevent unauthorized cross-origin requests, reducing the risk of CSRF attacks.

Comprehensive CSRF protection also involves secure coding practices. Developers should validate and sanitize all user inputs to prevent malicious data from reaching the application's core logic. Input validation and output encoding help protect against common vulnerabilities, such as SQL injection and cross-site scripting (XSS).

In addition, error handling and logging should be implemented carefully to prevent the exposure of sensitive information during CSRF attacks. Error messages should not reveal details about the application's internal structure or potential vulnerabilities. Logs should be generated and monitored for security-related events, enabling timely detection and response to CSRF incidents.

It is important to recognize that comprehensive CSRF protection is an ongoing process. Regular security assessments, including penetration testing and vulnerability scanning, can help identify and remediate CSRF vulnerabilities. Organizations should also stay informed about the latest security updates and patches for third-party components and libraries used in their applications.

Furthermore, security education and awareness programs for developers, administrators, and end-users are vital components of CSRF protection. Educating all stakeholders about the risks and mitigation techniques associated with CSRF attacks can help create a security-conscious culture within an organization.

Finally, continuous monitoring and incident response plans are essential for comprehensive CSRF protection. Monitoring for suspicious or anomalous activity can help detect CSRF attacks in real-time. Having well-defined incident response procedures ensures that organizations can respond swiftly and effectively when CSRF incidents occur.

In summary, comprehensive CSRF protection strategies encompass a combination of measures, including the use of anti-CSRF tokens, enforcing the SameSite attribute for cookies, implementing strong authentication and session management, configuring CORS policies correctly, secure coding practices, error handling and logging, regular security assessments, security education and awareness, and continuous monitoring and incident response. By adopting these strategies and practices, organizations can fortify their web applications against CSRF attacks and enhance overall security.

Chapter 9: Continuous Monitoring and Incident Response

Building a continuous security monitoring system is an essential component of maintaining the security of any organization's digital assets. Such a system provides real-time visibility into potential security threats, enabling swift response and mitigation. Next, we will explore the key elements and best practices for establishing an effective continuous security monitoring system.

The first step in building a continuous security monitoring system is defining your organization's security objectives and requirements. Understanding what assets need protection, the potential threats they face, and the regulatory or compliance standards that apply is crucial. These considerations will shape the design and scope of your monitoring system.

Next, you need to identify the data sources that will provide the necessary information for monitoring. These sources can include network logs, system logs, application logs, intrusion detection systems, antivirus software, and more. Having a comprehensive list of data sources ensures that your monitoring system can detect a wide range of security events.

To collect and centralize data from these sources, you'll need a Security Information and Event Management (SIEM) system or a similar solution. A SIEM platform aggregates and correlates data from various sources, providing a unified view of security events. It also allows for real-time analysis and alerts based on predefined rules and patterns.

Configuring your SIEM system to collect the right data and setting up meaningful alerts is critical. You should establish clear thresholds and criteria for when an event should trigger an alert. This prevents alert fatigue and ensures that your security team focuses on genuinely suspicious activity.

In addition to real-time alerts, a continuous security monitoring system should provide historical data analysis. This historical data can be valuable for identifying long-term trends and patterns that might indicate a security issue. It's also essential for incident response and forensic investigations.

Automated incident response is another essential element of a robust monitoring system. When an alert is triggered, automated actions can be taken to contain or mitigate the threat. These actions might include isolating a compromised device, blocking malicious IP addresses, or applying temporary access controls.

Regularly reviewing and updating your monitoring system's configurations and rules is crucial. New threats and attack techniques emerge regularly, so your system needs to adapt to these changes. Conducting regular security assessments and penetration testing can help identify weaknesses in your monitoring system and improve its effectiveness.

Integrating threat intelligence feeds into your monitoring system can enhance its capabilities. Threat intelligence provides information about the latest threats and vulnerabilities. By incorporating this information into your monitoring system, you can proactively identify potential risks and vulnerabilities within your organization.

User and entity behavior analytics (UEBA) can help detect insider threats and anomalous behavior. By monitoring user and entity activity, UEBA can identify deviations from normal behavior patterns, indicating potential insider threats or compromised accounts.

Continuous monitoring also extends to physical security. Monitoring access to sensitive areas, surveillance cameras, and environmental sensors can provide valuable insights into physical security breaches or incidents.

A critical aspect of building a continuous security monitoring system is ensuring that your organization has the necessary skills and expertise to operate it effectively. Training and developing a skilled security team is essential for the success of your monitoring efforts. Security professionals should be able to interpret alerts, investigate incidents, and respond to security events promptly.

An often-overlooked aspect of security monitoring is the need for a well-defined incident response plan. This plan should outline the steps to take when a security incident occurs, including communication procedures, containment strategies, and post-incident analysis. Regularly testing and updating the incident response plan ensures that your team is prepared for various scenarios.

Incorporating threat hunting as part of your monitoring strategy can help proactively identify threats that may not trigger automated alerts. Threat hunters use their expertise to actively search for signs of compromise or suspicious activity within the network. This proactive approach can uncover hidden threats that might go unnoticed by automated systems.

Finally, compliance with regulatory standards and data protection laws is essential when building a continuous security monitoring system. Ensure that your monitoring practices align with relevant compliance requirements, and that you maintain proper documentation to demonstrate compliance.

In summary, building a continuous security monitoring system is a multifaceted process that requires careful planning, the right technology, skilled personnel, and a commitment to ongoing improvement. By implementing these key elements and best practices, organizations can enhance their security posture and respond effectively to emerging threats.

Incident response is a critical component of web application security, ensuring that organizations can react swiftly and effectively when security incidents occur. Next, we will explore the key principles and best practices for effective incident response in web application security.

The first commandment of incident response is to have a well-defined incident response plan in place. This plan should outline the steps to take when a security incident is detected, from initial identification to containment, eradication, recovery, and lessons learned. Without a plan, chaos can ensue, and critical time can be lost in the event of an incident.

One of the fundamental principles of incident response is preparation. Preparation involves assembling an incident response team consisting of individuals with specific roles and responsibilities. This team should include incident handlers, communicators, technical experts, and legal and compliance personnel. Training and regular drills are essential to ensure that the team is prepared to respond effectively to various scenarios.

When an incident is detected, the first command is to initiate the incident response process immediately. Time is of the essence in mitigating the impact of an incident. The incident response team should be activated, and the incident should be properly categorized and prioritized based on its severity and potential impact.

Another critical principle is containment. The command here is to isolate the affected systems or components to prevent further damage or data loss. This might involve disconnecting compromised servers from the network, disabling compromised accounts, or blocking malicious IP addresses.

Gathering evidence is a crucial aspect of incident response. The command here is to preserve as much information as possible about the incident. This includes logs, system snapshots, network captures, and any other relevant data. Preserving evidence is essential for forensic analysis, identifying the root cause, and potentially prosecuting the perpetrators.

Transparency and communication are vital during incident response. The command here is to keep all stakeholders informed about the incident's status and impact. This includes senior management, legal, compliance, affected customers, and regulatory authorities. Clear and accurate communication helps manage the organization's reputation and builds trust with customers.

A critical command in incident response is to engage with external experts or authorities when necessary. In some cases, organizations may need to collaborate with law enforcement agencies, forensic experts, or cybersecurity firms. These external resources can provide valuable assistance in investigating and mitigating complex incidents.

Throughout the incident response process, documentation is essential. The command here is to maintain detailed records of all actions taken, decisions made, and evidence collected. Well-documented incident reports are valuable for post-incident analysis, legal proceedings, and compliance requirements.

After containment and eradication, the recovery phase begins. The command here is to restore affected systems and services to their normal operation. This may involve rebuilding compromised servers, applying patches, and strengthening security controls to prevent a recurrence.

Lessons learned from the incident are a crucial part of the incident response process. The command here is to conduct a thorough post-incident analysis to identify weaknesses in the organization's security posture and incident response procedures. These lessons can inform future security improvements and help prevent similar incidents.

Continuous improvement is a fundamental principle of incident response. The command here is to regularly review and update the incident response plan and procedures based on the lessons learned from past incidents and changes in the threat landscape. Incident response is an evolving discipline, and organizations must adapt to emerging threats and challenges.

A final command in effective incident response is to prioritize the well-being and support of the incident response team. Responding to security incidents can be stressful and demanding, and the team's morale and mental health should not be overlooked. Providing support and recognition for their efforts is essential for sustaining a strong incident response capability.

In summary, effective incident response in web application security is a well-orchestrated process that requires careful planning, training, and execution. By following the key principles and best practices outlined Next, organizations can respond swiftly and effectively to security incidents, minimize damage, and enhance their overall security posture.

Chapter 10: Application Security at Scale: DevSecOps and Beyond

Integrating security into DevOps practices is a fundamental shift in how organizations approach software development and deployment. This transformation recognizes that security should not be a separate and isolated process but an integral part of the entire software development lifecycle. One of the primary commands in this paradigm shift is to break down the traditional silos between development, operations, and security teams.

The DevOps approach emphasizes collaboration and communication, and integrating security seamlessly into this process is crucial. Developers, operations personnel, and security experts must work together from the early stages of development to ensure that security considerations are incorporated into every aspect of the software's design and deployment.

A key command when integrating security into DevOps practices is to implement security as code. This means that security controls, policies, and configurations are expressed as code and managed within the same version control system used for the application's source code. This enables security to be automated, versioned, and tested just like the application code.

Automation is a central theme in DevOps, and it applies equally to security. The command here is to automate security testing, vulnerability scanning, and compliance checks as part of the continuous integration and continuous delivery (CI/CD) pipeline. Automated security checks ensure that every code change is evaluated for security vulnerabilities before deployment.

Another critical command in integrating security into DevOps is to adopt a "shift left" mentality. This means moving security activities earlier in the development process. Security considerations should be present from the moment a new feature or functionality is planned, rather than being addressed as an afterthought.

Implementing security awareness and training for all team members is a crucial command. Developers, operations personnel, and security experts should have a shared understanding of security principles and best practices. This ensures that security is not perceived as a roadblock but as an enabler of secure and efficient software delivery.

A command that aligns with DevOps principles is to use infrastructure as code (IAC) for managing and provisioning resources. With IAC, security configurations can be defined alongside infrastructure definitions, making it easier to enforce security policies consistently across all environments, from development to production.

Implementing a process of continuous monitoring is essential in DevOps. The command here is to monitor not only the application's performance but also its security posture. Continuous security monitoring helps identify and address vulnerabilities and threats in real-time, reducing the risk of security incidents.

Integration of security into DevOps also requires a command to establish clear security metrics and key performance indicators (KPIs). These metrics help organizations measure the effectiveness of their security practices and identify areas for improvement. Metrics can include the number of vulnerabilities detected and remediated, mean time to detect and respond to incidents, and compliance with security policies.

One of the most critical commands in integrating security into DevOps is to conduct regular security assessments and penetration testing. Security assessments help identify vulnerabilities and weaknesses in both the application and infrastructure. These assessments should be conducted throughout the development process and during the production phase.

Implementing secure coding practices is another essential command. Developers should be trained to write code that is resistant to common security vulnerabilities, such as injection attacks, cross-site scripting (XSS), and authentication bypass. Secure coding guidelines and automated code analysis tools can help enforce these practices.

A command that aligns with the concept of immutable infrastructure is to rebuild or redeploy compromised components rather than attempting to remediate them. This approach minimizes the risk of persistent threats and ensures that known vulnerabilities are not carried forward.

A key command when integrating security into DevOps is to establish a clear incident response plan specifically tailored to the DevOps environment. This plan should define roles and responsibilities for incident response within the DevOps team and outline procedures for identifying, containing, and recovering from security incidents.

Integrating security into DevOps practices also requires organizations to engage with external security experts and threat intelligence sources. The command here is to stay informed about the latest threats and vulnerabilities that may impact the organization's applications and infrastructure. External expertise can provide valuable insights and recommendations for improving security practices.

Finally, integrating security into DevOps is an ongoing process. The command here is to continually assess and refine security practices to adapt to changing threats and evolving technology. Continuous improvement ensures that security remains a core component of the DevOps culture and contributes to the organization's overall success.

In summary, integrating security into DevOps practices is a transformative shift that requires a change in mindset, collaboration, and automation. By following the commands outlined Next, organizations can build a culture of security that is integrated seamlessly into the DevOps pipeline, resulting in more secure and resilient applications.

Scaling application security efforts for large systems is a complex undertaking that demands a comprehensive strategy and a clear set of commands. In large-scale systems, the attack surface is broader, and the potential impact of security vulnerabilities can be significant, making it crucial to prioritize security. One of the key commands in this context is to establish a dedicated application security team or center of excellence.

This team should consist of security experts with specialized knowledge in application security. Their primary responsibility is to develop and implement security policies, guidelines, and best practices tailored to the organization's unique needs. Having a dedicated team focused on application security ensures that security concerns are consistently addressed throughout the organization's software development lifecycle.

Another command is to adopt a risk-based approach to prioritize security efforts. Not all parts of a large system are equally critical, and resources should be allocated based on the potential impact of a security breach. This approach allows organizations to focus their efforts on protecting the most sensitive and valuable assets.

In large systems, a command that aligns with DevSecOps principles is to automate security testing and vulnerability scanning. Automation enables organizations to conduct regular security assessments across a vast and dynamic application landscape. Automated tools can identify vulnerabilities, misconfigurations, and compliance issues, allowing teams to remediate them promptly.

Implementing security orchestration and incident response automation (SOAR) is another critical command. SOAR platforms can streamline incident detection and response by automating repetitive tasks and workflows. In large systems, security incidents can occur frequently, and SOAR can help reduce response times and minimize the impact of incidents.

A command related to threat modeling is to conduct a thorough analysis of the entire system. Large systems are complex, and understanding their architecture, data flow, and dependencies is crucial for identifying potential security risks. Threat modeling helps organizations prioritize security measures and allocate resources effectively.

A command that complements threat modeling is to establish strong access controls. Large systems often have multiple user roles and permissions, and it's essential to implement fine-grained access controls to limit privileges based on the principle of least privilege. This command helps mitigate the risk of unauthorized access and data breaches.

In large systems, it's vital to implement continuous monitoring and logging. The command here is to have a robust monitoring infrastructure in place to detect suspicious activities and anomalies. Logs should be collected and analyzed centrally to provide visibility into the security status of the entire system.

A critical command for large systems is to implement a robust identity and access management (IAM) system. IAM ensures that users and services have appropriate access to resources and data. Organizations should enforce strong authentication methods, implement multi-factor authentication (MFA), and regularly review and update access policies.

Secure coding practices are essential, and the command is to educate developers and enforce coding standards. Large systems involve numerous developers and code contributors, making it essential to establish consistent coding practices that prioritize security. Code reviews and automated code analysis tools can help identify and remediate security vulnerabilities.

A command that aligns with the principle of least privilege is to regularly review and audit permissions and access rights. Large systems often accumulate unnecessary permissions over time, increasing the attack surface. Regular reviews and audits ensure that access rights are aligned with current business requirements and security policies.

Implementing secure software development lifecycle (SDLC) practices is a crucial command. Large systems require a structured approach to development and testing, with security integrated at every stage. Security assessments, code reviews, and penetration testing should be part of the SDLC to identify and address vulnerabilities proactively.

A command that addresses third-party risk management is to conduct thorough due diligence on external dependencies. Large systems may rely on third-party libraries, APIs, and services. Organizations should assess the security practices of third-party providers and have a process for evaluating and monitoring their security posture.

In large systems, incident response planning is critical, and the command is to establish an incident response team with defined roles and procedures. Large systems may experience a wide range of security incidents, from data breaches to service disruptions. Having a well-prepared incident response team ensures a coordinated and effective response to mitigate the impact.

The command to establish a comprehensive security training and awareness program is vital. In large organizations, employees at all levels should receive regular security training to recognize and report security threats. Awareness programs help create a security-conscious culture throughout the organization.

An essential command is to conduct regular security drills and simulations. Large systems can be targets of sophisticated attacks, and organizations must be prepared to respond effectively. Security drills help test incident response procedures and improve the team's readiness.

A command that addresses supply chain security is to assess and secure the entire software supply chain. Large systems often rely on a complex ecosystem of suppliers and partners. Organizations should evaluate the security practices of suppliers, monitor the integrity of software components, and establish mechanisms for rapid response to supply chain incidents.

A command that aligns with compliance requirements is to maintain comprehensive documentation of security policies, procedures, and compliance efforts. Large organizations often have regulatory obligations, and documentation is critical for audits and demonstrating compliance.

In summary, scaling application security efforts for large systems is a multifaceted challenge. By following the commands outlined Next, organizations can establish a robust security posture that safeguards their critical assets, mitigates risks, and ensures the resilience of large-scale systems in the face of evolving threats.

BOOK 4
THE ULTIMATE OWASP TOP 10 HANDBOOK
EXPERT INSIGHTS AND MITIGATION STRATEGIES

ROB BOTWRIGHT

Chapter 1: Demystifying the OWASP Top 10

To understand the origins of the OWASP Top 10, we need to delve into the history of web application security. The Open Web Application Security Project, or OWASP, is a nonprofit organization dedicated to improving the security of web applications. The OWASP Top 10 is a list of the most critical web application security risks, first published in 2003. The command here is to explore the factors that led to the creation of the OWASP Top 10 and its evolution over the years.

In the early 2000s, as web applications became increasingly prevalent, so did the number of security vulnerabilities and attacks targeting them. Organizations were facing a growing challenge in securing their web applications, and there was a lack of standardized guidance on the most critical security risks. Recognizing this gap, the OWASP community initiated the development of a list that would serve as a reference for web application security.

The initial version of the OWASP Top 10 was released in 2003, and it aimed to provide a concise and prioritized list of common web application vulnerabilities. The command here was to identify the vulnerabilities that posed the greatest risk to web applications and their users. The list was intended to be a valuable resource for developers, security professionals, and organizations seeking to secure their web applications effectively.

The first OWASP Top 10 consisted of vulnerabilities such as SQL injection, cross-site scripting (XSS), and insecure authentication and session management. These vulnerabilities were considered some of the most prevalent and damaging at the time. The command was to highlight these risks and raise awareness within the industry.

Over the years, the OWASP Top 10 evolved to reflect changes in the threat landscape and advancements in web application security. The command was to regularly update the list to ensure that it remained relevant and reflected the current state of web application security. New versions of the OWASP Top 10 were released to address emerging threats and provide guidance on mitigating them effectively.

One significant aspect of the OWASP Top 10 is that it is based on real-world data and input from security experts. The command here is to gather data on security incidents, breaches, and vulnerabilities to inform the selection of the top risks. The list is not purely theoretical; it is grounded in the practical experiences of the security community.

The OWASP Top 10 is not static; it adapts to changes in technology and attack techniques. The command is to stay ahead of the evolving threat landscape and provide timely guidance to organizations. This flexibility has allowed the OWASP Top 10 to remain a valuable resource for web application security.

The OWASP community has always encouraged feedback and contributions from the broader security community. The command here is to promote collaboration and knowledge-sharing among experts and practitioners. By involving a diverse range of perspectives, the OWASP Top 10 can better address the multifaceted nature of web application security.

Each new version of the OWASP Top 10 incorporates feedback and insights from experts and organizations worldwide. The command is to ensure that the list is a collective effort, reflecting the global nature of web application security challenges. This collaborative approach enhances the list's accuracy and relevance.

The OWASP Top 10 serves as a benchmark for organizations to assess their web application security posture. The command here is to use the list as a starting point for evaluating vulnerabilities and risks in their applications. By aligning their security efforts with the OWASP Top 10, organizations can focus on addressing the most critical threats first.

In addition to helping organizations prioritize security efforts, the OWASP Top 10 has influenced industry standards and regulations. The command is to recognize the list's significance in shaping best practices and compliance requirements. Many organizations and regulatory bodies refer to the OWASP Top 10 when developing security guidelines and requirements for web applications.

The OWASP Top 10 has become a well-known and respected resource in the field of web application security. The command here is to continue promoting awareness and adoption of the list. Educational materials, training programs, and community events centered around the OWASP Top 10 have contributed to its widespread recognition.

In summary, the origins of the OWASP Top 10 can be traced back to the need for a standardized and prioritized list of web application security risks. The command to address this need has led to the creation and evolution of the OWASP Top 10, which continues to play a crucial role in enhancing web application security worldwide.

To grasp the significance of the OWASP Top 10, it's essential to recognize the critical role it plays in the realm of web application security. The command here is to delve into the reasons why the OWASP Top 10 is a cornerstone of web security practices. Web applications have become an integral part of modern life, powering everything from online banking to e-commerce platforms and social media networks. The command is to understand that these applications process vast amounts of sensitive data, making them attractive targets for malicious actors seeking to exploit vulnerabilities.

One fundamental aspect of web application security is the constant threat of attacks, which can have severe consequences for organizations and individuals alike. The command here is to acknowledge that these attacks can lead to data breaches, financial losses, reputational damage, and legal liabilities. To mitigate these risks, it's crucial to identify and address the most prevalent and impactful security vulnerabilities effectively.

The OWASP Top 10 provides a standardized framework for achieving this goal. The command is to recognize the list as a valuable tool for understanding and prioritizing web application security risks. One of the core strengths of the OWASP Top 10 is its simplicity and accessibility. The command here is to appreciate its straightforward format, which presents the ten most critical vulnerabilities in a concise and comprehensible manner.

This simplicity allows a wide range of stakeholders, from developers to executives, to grasp the key security threats facing web applications. The command is to leverage this accessibility to foster collaboration and communication among different teams within an organization. For example, developers can use the OWASP Top 10 as a reference to understand security requirements, while security professionals can use it to communicate risk effectively.

Moreover, the OWASP Top 10 serves as a common language for discussing web application security across the industry. The command here is to understand that this common language facilitates knowledge sharing and collaboration among security professionals, researchers, and organizations. It enables the security community to discuss emerging threats, share mitigation strategies, and develop best practices that benefit the entire ecosystem.

The OWASP Top 10 also provides a framework for risk assessment and prioritization. The command is to recognize its role in helping organizations allocate limited resources effectively. By focusing on the vulnerabilities listed in the OWASP Top 10, organizations can address the most critical security risks first, reducing their exposure to potential threats.

Additionally, the OWASP Top 10 encourages proactive security measures. The command here is to understand that it's not merely a list of vulnerabilities but a guide for building robust security into the software development lifecycle. Developers and security teams can use the OWASP Top 10 to implement security controls, conduct security testing, and follow best practices that help prevent vulnerabilities from occurring in the first place.

The OWASP Top 10 evolves to keep pace with the ever-changing landscape of web application security. The command is to stay updated with new versions and revisions of the list to remain informed about emerging threats. This adaptability ensures that the OWASP Top 10 remains a relevant and reliable resource for addressing current security challenges.

Furthermore, the OWASP Top 10 is a valuable resource for security training and education. The command here is to leverage it to educate developers, security professionals, and other stakeholders about the importance of web application security. Training programs and courses that incorporate the OWASP Top 10 can help individuals and teams acquire the knowledge and skills needed to build and maintain secure web applications.

The OWASP community actively encourages contributions and feedback from the security community. The command is to participate in this collaborative effort by sharing insights, research findings, and real-world experiences. Contributions help improve the accuracy and relevance of the OWASP Top 10, making it an even more valuable resource for the community.

The list is not static; it reflects the evolving nature of web application security. The command here is to recognize that new threats and attack techniques constantly emerge. The OWASP community and experts worldwide continuously assess and update the list to ensure that it reflects the current threat landscape.

Organizations that align their security practices with the OWASP Top 10 can gain a competitive advantage. The command is to understand that prioritizing web application security enhances an organization's reputation, builds trust with customers, and reduces the likelihood of costly security incidents. By following the guidance provided in the OWASP Top 10, organizations can demonstrate their commitment to safeguarding user data and delivering secure web experiences.

In summary, the importance of the OWASP Top 10 cannot be overstated in the context of web application security. The command here is to embrace it as a foundational resource that empowers organizations to identify, address, and mitigate the most critical web application vulnerabilities. By recognizing its significance and incorporating its principles into security practices, organizations can bolster their defenses against evolving threats and provide a safer online environment for users.

Chapter 2: Injection Attacks: Advanced Analysis and Mitigation

In the realm of web application security, advanced injection attack techniques pose a formidable challenge that demands a deeper understanding. The command here is to delve into the intricacies of these techniques to appreciate their complexity and potential impact. Injection attacks, such as SQL injection and Command injection, have been a persistent threat to web applications for many years. The command is to recognize their ability to manipulate data, execute unauthorized commands, and compromise the confidentiality, integrity, and availability of data and systems.

To analyze advanced injection attack techniques, it's essential to first comprehend the fundamental principles behind injection vulnerabilities. The command here is to establish a solid foundation by understanding how these vulnerabilities occur and why they are so exploitable. Injection vulnerabilities typically arise when untrusted data is incorporated into a command or query without proper validation or sanitization. The command is to grasp that attackers leverage this vulnerability to inject malicious input, effectively tricking the application into executing unintended commands.

One of the most well-known injection attack types is SQL injection. The command here is to explore this attack in-depth to uncover its nuances and countermeasures. In SQL injection attacks, malicious input is inserted into SQL queries, leading to unauthorized access to the database or the ability to manipulate data within it. The command is to comprehend that attackers can extract sensitive information, modify data, or even gain administrative privileges through SQL injection.

Advanced SQL injection techniques often involve blind injection and time-based attacks. The command here is to appreciate the sophistication of these techniques, which make it challenging to detect and mitigate SQL injection. In blind SQL injection, attackers infer information indirectly by observing the application's behavior. The command is to understand that time-based attacks introduce delays in SQL queries to reveal information gradually, making them harder to detect.

Command injection is another prevalent type of injection attack that targets system commands. The command here is to delve into the intricacies of command injection and its potential impact. In command injection attacks, untrusted input is passed to system commands, enabling attackers to execute arbitrary commands on the underlying server. The command is to recognize that this can lead to remote code execution, data exfiltration, or even the complete compromise of the server.

To mitigate advanced injection attacks, it's crucial to implement proper input validation and output encoding. The command here is to emphasize the importance of input validation to ensure that only valid and expected data is accepted. Input validation involves validating data types, length, format, and range to prevent malicious input from being processed. The command is to understand that output encoding helps ensure that data is correctly displayed in web applications, preventing attackers from injecting malicious code.

Web application firewalls (WAFs) can also be employed to detect and block injection attacks. The command here is to recognize WAFs as an additional layer of defense that can identify and mitigate attacks in real-time. WAFs use predefined rules and heuristics to identify patterns associated with injection attacks and block malicious requests. The command is to understand that while WAFs are a valuable tool, they should be used in conjunction with other security measures for comprehensive protection.

Parameterized queries and prepared statements are effective techniques for preventing SQL injection. The command here is to appreciate the role of these techniques in securing database interactions. Parameterized queries ensure that user input is treated as data, not executable code, reducing the risk of SQL injection. The command is to understand that prepared statements separate SQL code from user input, making it virtually impossible for attackers to inject malicious SQL.

To defend against command injection, it's essential to adopt secure coding practices and avoid executing system commands with user-controlled input. The command here is to recognize the significance of code review and secure development methodologies. Developers should follow secure coding guidelines, use safe APIs, and validate all input data rigorously. The command is to understand that minimizing the use of system commands that incorporate user input can also reduce the attack surface.

In addition to technical defenses, user education is crucial in mitigating injection attacks. The command here is to emphasize the role of security awareness training in fostering a security-conscious culture. Users should be educated about the risks of injection attacks, phishing attempts, and the importance of strong authentication. The command is to understand that informed users can be the first line of defense against social engineering and injection attacks.

Regular security testing, including vulnerability scanning and penetration testing, is essential for identifying and remediating injection vulnerabilities. The command here is to incorporate these practices into the development lifecycle to proactively identify and address security weaknesses. Vulnerability scanning tools can automatically detect common injection vulnerabilities, while penetration testing involves manual testing by security experts. The command is to comprehend that a combination of automated and manual testing provides a comprehensive assessment of an application's security posture.

In summary, advanced injection attack techniques represent a persistent and evolving threat to web applications. The command here is to recognize the complexity of these attacks and the potential harm they can inflict. To defend against advanced injection attacks effectively, organizations must adopt a multi-layered security approach that encompasses input validation, output encoding, secure coding practices, and user education. By understanding the nuances of these attack techniques and implementing robust defenses, organizations can significantly reduce their vulnerability to injection attacks and enhance their overall web application security.

In the ever-evolving landscape of web application security,

advanced mitigation strategies for injection attacks are essential to combat increasingly sophisticated threats. The command here is to explore these strategies in-depth to understand their effectiveness and implementation. Injection attacks, such as SQL injection and Command injection, continue to pose a significant risk to web applications. The command is to recognize that attackers exploit vulnerabilities to manipulate data, execute unauthorized commands, and compromise the integrity and availability of systems.

To effectively mitigate injection attacks, organizations must adopt a multi-faceted approach that combines various defensive measures. The command here is to emphasize that relying solely on one defense mechanism may leave vulnerabilities unaddressed. One of the fundamental strategies for mitigating injection attacks is input validation and sanitization. The command is to understand that this process involves examining and cleansing user input to ensure it adheres to expected data types, formats, and ranges.

Input validation helps prevent malicious input from reaching critical application components, thereby reducing the risk of injection attacks. The command here is to appreciate its role as the first line of defense against potential threats. Implementing robust input validation requires thorough examination of each input source, including form fields, URL parameters, and cookies. The command is to understand that different inputs may require specific validation rules to ensure comprehensive coverage.

Another crucial strategy is the use of parameterized queries and prepared statements when interacting with databases. The command here is to recognize their importance in preventing SQL injection attacks. Parameterized queries and prepared statements separate user input from SQL code execution, making it nearly impossible for attackers to inject malicious SQL commands.

Parameterized queries bind user input to placeholders in the query, ensuring that input is treated as data, not code. The command is to understand that this practice significantly reduces the risk of SQL injection. Prepared statements, on the other hand, compile the query separately from user input, providing even stronger protection. The command is to appreciate their role in maintaining security when interacting with databases.

In addition to input validation and database protection, output encoding is a critical component of injection attack mitigation. The command here is to recognize that output encoding safeguards against attacks that attempt to inject malicious code into the application's responses. Output encoding ensures that user-generated content is displayed as data, not executable code, thereby thwarting attempts to execute scripts or inject malicious payloads.

Web application firewalls (WAFs) are valuable tools in the fight against injection attacks. The command is to understand that WAFs act as a protective barrier between web applications and potential attackers. They use predefined rules and heuristics to detect and block malicious traffic, including injection attempts. The command is to appreciate the real-time protection they offer and their ability to identify patterns associated with injection attacks.

However, organizations should use WAFs as part of a layered security strategy, not as the sole defense mechanism. The command here is to comprehend that WAFs complement other security measures and should be integrated into a comprehensive security posture. Regular monitoring and tuning of WAFs are necessary to ensure they effectively identify and block injection attacks while minimizing false positives.

Security testing, including vulnerability scanning and penetration testing, plays a crucial role in identifying and remediating injection vulnerabilities. The command is to incorporate these practices into the development lifecycle to proactively identify and address security weaknesses. Vulnerability scanning tools automatically detect common injection vulnerabilities, while penetration testing involves manual testing by security experts. The command is to understand that a combination of automated and manual testing provides a comprehensive assessment of an application's security posture.

Intrusion detection and prevention systems (IDPS) can also enhance the organization's ability to detect and respond to injection attacks. The command is to recognize the value of IDPS in monitoring network traffic for suspicious patterns and signatures associated with known attacks. IDPS can alert security teams to potential injection attempts, enabling them to respond promptly and investigate further.

Education and training are vital components of a robust security strategy. The command here is to emphasize the role of security awareness training in building a security-conscious culture. Employees and developers should be educated about the risks of injection attacks and the importance of secure coding practices. The command is to understand that informed users and development teams can contribute significantly to reducing the likelihood of successful injection attacks.

In summary, advanced mitigation strategies for injection attacks are essential in safeguarding web applications against evolving threats. The command here is to recognize that no single defense mechanism can provide complete protection. Organizations must adopt a comprehensive approach that includes input validation, output encoding, parameterized queries, prepared statements, WAFs, security testing, IDPS, and user education.

By implementing these strategies in combination, organizations can significantly reduce their vulnerability to injection attacks and enhance their overall web application security. The command is to appreciate the complexity of injection attacks and the importance of staying vigilant in the face of ever-evolving threats.

Chapter 3: Fortifying Authentication and Session Management

In the realm of web application security, advanced authentication techniques are crucial components of a robust defense strategy. The command here is to delve into these techniques to understand their significance and potential impact. Authentication is the process by which a system verifies the identity of users, ensuring they have the appropriate permissions and access to resources. The command is to recognize that effective authentication is fundamental to preventing unauthorized access and protecting sensitive data.

One of the advanced authentication techniques gaining prominence is Multi-Factor Authentication (MFA). The command here is to explore MFA in detail to appreciate its role in enhancing security. MFA adds an extra layer of protection by requiring users to provide two or more forms of authentication before granting access. The command is to understand that this could include something the user knows (like a password), something the user has (like a smartphone), and something the user is (like a fingerprint).

The beauty of MFA lies in its ability to thwart attackers, even if they have stolen a user's password. The command here is to emphasize the effectiveness of MFA in mitigating the risks of credential theft. Even if an attacker possesses a user's password, they would still need access to the second factor, which could be a mobile app, a security token, or a biometric identifier. The command is to comprehend that this added layer of security significantly reduces the likelihood of unauthorized access. Biometric authentication is another advanced technique that leverages unique physical or behavioral characteristics for identity verification. The command here is to delve into biometric authentication to understand its strengths and limitations. Biometrics can include fingerprint recognition, facial recognition, iris scanning, and even voice recognition. The command is to appreciate that these methods provide a highly personalized and secure way to confirm a user's identity.

One of the advantages of biometric authentication is that it's challenging for attackers to replicate or forge biometric data. The command here is to recognize that this makes it a robust authentication method for securing access to sensitive systems. However, it's essential to note that biometric data must be securely stored and processed to prevent potential privacy and security concerns. The command is to understand that compromised biometric data can't be easily changed, making its protection paramount.

Adaptive authentication is another advanced technique that assesses user behavior and risk factors in real-time. The command here is to explore adaptive authentication to grasp its dynamic nature. Adaptive authentication uses contextual information, such as location, device, and behavior patterns, to determine the level of authentication required. The command is to comprehend that this approach adapts to the current risk environment, providing a more nuanced and responsive security posture.

One of the key benefits of adaptive authentication is its ability to balance security and user experience. The command here is to recognize that it minimizes friction for legitimate users while imposing additional security measures when unusual or high-risk activities are detected. For example, if a user logs in from their usual location and device, they may only need a password. The command is to understand that if they attempt to log in from an unfamiliar location or device, adaptive authentication may prompt for additional verification.

Time-based one-time passwords (TOTP) and hardware security tokens are also advanced authentication methods. The command here is to explore these techniques to understand their role in enhancing security. TOTP involves generating a unique, time-sensitive code using a mobile app or a dedicated device. The command is to appreciate that this code is valid only for a short period, making it challenging for attackers to reuse.

Hardware security tokens, on the other hand, are physical devices that generate one-time codes or provide cryptographic keys. The command is to understand that these tokens add an extra layer of security by requiring users to possess the physical device. These tokens are particularly valuable for securing critical systems and resources.

Role-based authentication is another advanced technique that grants access based on specific roles or privileges. The command here is to explore role-based authentication to grasp its flexibility. In role-based authentication, users are assigned roles with predefined permissions. The command is to recognize that users can access resources and perform actions based on their assigned roles.

One of the advantages of role-based authentication is its fine-grained control over access. The command here is to appreciate that it allows organizations to enforce the principle of least privilege, ensuring that users only have access to what's necessary for their roles. This reduces the risk of unauthorized access and data breaches.

To implement advanced authentication techniques effectively, organizations must consider several factors. The command here is to emphasize that a thoughtful strategy and careful implementation are essential. First and foremost, a risk assessment should be conducted to identify the appropriate level of authentication for different scenarios. The command is to understand that not all systems or resources require the same level of security, and a risk-based approach can help allocate resources wisely.

User education and awareness are also crucial aspects of advanced authentication. The command here is to recognize that users play a vital role in the security chain. They must understand the importance of following best practices, such as protecting their authentication credentials and using MFA when available. The command is to understand that even the most advanced authentication methods can be compromised if users are not vigilant.

Integration with identity and access management (IAM) systems is essential for managing and enforcing advanced authentication policies. The command here is to appreciate that IAM solutions provide centralized control over user identities, roles, and access permissions. They also facilitate the seamless integration of various authentication methods, making it easier to implement MFA, biometrics, adaptive authentication, and role-based access control.

Session management is a critical aspect of web application security, and robust strategies are essential for protecting user sessions and sensitive data. The command here is to explore various strategies for enhancing session management in web applications to mitigate security risks effectively. A session, in the context of web applications, refers to the period during which a user interacts with the application after successfully logging in. The command is to understand that sessions are used to maintain user state and allow users to access various parts of the application without repeatedly authenticating.

One fundamental aspect of robust session management is session timeout settings. The command here is to recognize that defining appropriate session timeouts is crucial for security. Session timeouts determine how long a user's session remains active after their last interaction with the application. The command is to comprehend that setting excessively long session timeouts can increase the risk of unauthorized access if a user leaves their device unattended.

On the other hand, overly short session timeouts can lead to a poor user experience, as users may frequently need to re-authenticate. The command here is to emphasize the importance of striking the right balance based on the application's security requirements and user expectations. For example, a banking application may have shorter session timeouts to enhance security, while a news website might have longer timeouts to improve user convenience.

Another strategy for robust session management involves implementing secure session cookies. The command here is to explore the concept of session cookies and their role in security. Session cookies are unique identifiers sent by the server to the user's browser to associate subsequent requests with the user's session. The command is to understand that securing these cookies is vital to prevent session hijacking or theft.

Secure session cookies should be marked with the "HttpOnly" and "Secure" attributes. The command here is to delve into these attributes to grasp their significance. The "HttpOnly" attribute ensures that the cookie is inaccessible to JavaScript, reducing the risk of cross-site scripting (XSS) attacks. The command is to recognize that XSS attacks could potentially steal session cookies if they are not protected.

The "Secure" attribute, on the other hand, ensures that the cookie is transmitted only over secure HTTPS connections. The command here is to understand that this prevents attackers from intercepting the cookie during transit when users are accessing the application over unsecured HTTP.

Furthermore, implementing session fixation prevention measures is essential for robust session management. The command here is to explore session fixation and how to mitigate this type of attack. Session fixation occurs when an attacker sets a user's session identifier to a known value, allowing them to hijack the user's session. The command is to comprehend that this attack can be mitigated by regenerating the session identifier upon authentication.

Additionally, robust session management strategies should include protection against session fixation by checking the user's IP address or user agent for consistency. The command here is to understand that these checks can help detect suspicious changes in the user's environment, potentially indicating a session fixation attempt.

Session invalidation mechanisms are also crucial for enhancing session management. The command here is to explore session invalidation and its role in security. When a user logs out or their session times out, it's essential to invalidate the session and remove any associated session data. The command is to recognize that failing to do so could leave sensitive information accessible to unauthorized users.

Furthermore, implementing anti-CSRF tokens can help protect against Cross-Site Request Forgery (CSRF) attacks that target user sessions. The command here is to delve into CSRF attacks and the importance of anti-CSRF tokens. CSRF attacks trick users into making unintended actions on an application where they are authenticated. The command is to understand that anti-CSRF tokens can prevent these attacks by ensuring that requests originate from the user's session and not from malicious sources.

It's important to emphasize the significance of strong session management controls in preventing session-related vulnerabilities. The command here is to understand that session-related vulnerabilities, if not addressed properly, can lead to unauthorized access, data breaches, and compromised user accounts. By implementing the mentioned strategies, organizations can strengthen their session management practices and provide a more secure experience for users.

Moreover, auditing and monitoring of session activities are essential components of robust session management. The command here is to explore the role of auditing and monitoring in session management. Logging session-related events, such as login attempts, session creations, and session terminations, can provide valuable insights into potential security threats and anomalies.

Regularly reviewing session logs and conducting security audits can help detect suspicious activities, such as multiple login failures or unauthorized access attempts. The command is to understand that early detection of such activities allows organizations to take proactive measures to mitigate potential threats.

Implementing session management policies and controls, such as password-based reauthentication for sensitive operations, can further enhance security. The command here is to delve into reauthentication and its role in session management. Reauthentication requires users to provide their password or another form of authentication before performing sensitive actions, such as changing account settings or accessing financial transactions.

This additional layer of security ensures that even if an attacker gains access to an active session, they cannot execute critical actions without reconfirming their identity. The command is to recognize that reauthentication can be particularly important for high-risk operations and privileged accounts.

Session management strategies should also consider the use of secure transport protocols, such as HTTPS. The command here is to emphasize the importance of using HTTPS to protect session data in transit. HTTPS encrypts the communication between the user's browser and the web server, safeguarding session-related information from eavesdroppers and man-in-the-middle attacks.

Organizations should regularly update and patch their web applications and session management components to address known vulnerabilities. The command here is to stress the significance of staying up-to-date with security patches and updates. Vulnerabilities in session management libraries or frameworks can be exploited by attackers to compromise sessions and gain unauthorized access.

Additionally, educating users about session security best practices can contribute to robust session management. The command here is to recognize that informed users are more likely to take precautions, such as logging out of shared computers and not saving passwords on public devices.

In summary, robust session management is a cornerstone of web application security, and implementing these strategies is essential for safeguarding user sessions and sensitive data. The command is to understand that by carefully considering session timeout settings, securing session cookies, preventing session fixation, implementing session invalidation mechanisms, and using anti-CSRF tokens, organizations can significantly reduce the risk of session-related vulnerabilities.

Auditing and monitoring session activities, enforcing reauthentication for sensitive operations, using secure transport protocols like HTTPS, keeping software components up-to-date, and educating users about session security best practices are equally vital elements of a comprehensive session management strategy.

By implementing these strategies, organizations can not only protect their users' sessions but also enhance the overall security posture of their web applications, ultimately providing a safer online experience for their users.

Chapter 4: Unmasking Cross-Site Scripting (XSS) Exploits

Understanding Cross-Site Scripting (XSS) vulnerabilities is crucial for comprehensive web application security. XSS attacks involve injecting malicious scripts into web pages viewed by other users. These scripts can steal sensitive information, manipulate user interactions, or even deface websites. In advanced XSS scenarios, attackers employ sophisticated techniques to evade detection and maximize the impact of their attacks. For instance, they may use obfuscation to hide malicious code within seemingly benign scripts or employ evasion techniques to bypass security filters.

One advanced method attackers use is DOM-based XSS. DOM-based XSS occurs when the browser's Document Object Model (DOM) is manipulated to execute malicious code. Unlike traditional XSS, where the server sends a response containing malicious scripts, DOM-based XSS involves client-side script execution. This can make it challenging to detect and mitigate.

In DOM-based XSS, an attacker manipulates the DOM to execute scripts, often by modifying the URL or user inputs. For example, an attacker could craft a URL that contains malicious code, and when a user clicks on the link, the code executes within their browser. Advanced attackers may use JavaScript functions and event handlers creatively to trigger the execution of malicious code.

Another advanced XSS technique is reflective XSS. In this scenario, the attacker injects malicious code that is immediately reflected off a web application and executed in the victim's browser. This can occur when an application fails to properly validate and sanitize user inputs. Attackers often exploit reflective XSS to steal user session cookies or perform actions on behalf of the victim. Stored XSS is another variant of XSS where the injected script is permanently stored on a web server. When a user visits a page that contains the injected script, it is executed in their browser. Advanced attackers may use stored XSS to distribute malware or perform targeted attacks on specific users.

XSS payloads can be obfuscated to avoid detection by security filters. This obfuscation involves encoding or transforming the script in ways that make it challenging for security tools to identify. Common obfuscation techniques include character encoding, using escape sequences, or encoding the payload in multiple layers.

For instance, an attacker might encode their payload using Base64 encoding, which looks like harmless text but can be decoded and executed by the browser. Advanced obfuscation techniques can make it challenging for security scanners and manual reviewers to identify and mitigate XSS vulnerabilities effectively.

Polyglot XSS is an advanced technique where a single payload works in multiple contexts or programming languages. This makes it even more difficult to defend against XSS attacks because the same payload can be used to exploit different vulnerabilities. For example, a polyglot XSS payload might be valid in both JavaScript and HTML, allowing it to execute in various scenarios.

Another advanced XSS variant is the use of Blind XSS. In Blind XSS, an attacker injects malicious code that is not immediately executed but is stored for later exploitation. This type of XSS is more challenging to detect because the attacker may not receive immediate feedback on whether the injection was successful. They rely on finding specific circumstances where the injected code will be executed in the future.

Challenges in mitigating advanced XSS attacks include the need for effective input validation and output encoding. Web applications must thoroughly validate and sanitize user inputs to prevent attackers from injecting malicious scripts. Additionally, output encoding should be applied consistently to ensure that any data rendered in the browser is safe from script injection.

Using Content Security Policy (CSP) headers is an advanced defense mechanism against XSS. CSP allows website owners to specify which sources of content are trusted and can be executed in the browser. This can help block the execution of malicious scripts, even if they are injected into the page.

Regular security testing, including manual code reviews and automated scanning, is essential for identifying and addressing XSS vulnerabilities. Security researchers and penetration testers often employ advanced tools and techniques to uncover XSS issues that might elude standard scans.

To protect against advanced XSS attacks, organizations should stay informed about emerging threats and vulnerabilities. They should also train developers and security teams to recognize and mitigate XSS risks effectively.

In summary, advanced insights into Cross-Site Scripting (XSS) vulnerabilities are crucial for modern web application security. Attackers continuously evolve their techniques, making it essential for defenders to stay one step ahead. Understanding advanced XSS variants, such as DOM-based XSS, reflective XSS, and stored XSS, as well as obfuscation and polyglot payloads, is vital for effective defense.

Implementing measures like Content Security Policy (CSP), robust input validation, output encoding, and regular security testing are key components of a comprehensive XSS defense strategy. By staying informed, training teams, and employing the right tools and techniques, organizations can better protect their web applications and users from the ever-evolving threat of XSS attacks.

Deconstructing complex Cross-Site Scripting (XSS) exploits is an essential skill for understanding the inner workings of sophisticated attacks. These exploits often involve multiple layers of obfuscation, manipulation, and evasion techniques, making them challenging to analyze. By breaking down these complex exploits step by step, security professionals can gain valuable insights into attacker methodologies and develop more robust defensive strategies.

Complex XSS exploits typically start with an attacker identifying a vulnerable web application. This vulnerability may be a result of inadequate input validation or output encoding, which allows the injection of malicious scripts into the application's response.

Once a vulnerable application is identified, the attacker crafts a payload containing JavaScript code that will execute in the victim's browser. This payload can range from simple scripts to highly sophisticated code designed to achieve specific goals, such as stealing user credentials or session cookies.

Obfuscation techniques are frequently employed to hide the malicious nature of the payload. These techniques make it difficult for security scanners and filters to detect the presence of malicious scripts. Obfuscation may involve encoding the payload using methods like Base64 or hexadecimal encoding, or using escape characters to evade detection.

To deliver the payload to the victim, the attacker often relies on social engineering tactics. This may include sending phishing emails with links to the malicious site or tricking users into clicking on infected advertisements or links.

Once the victim interacts with the malicious content, the payload is executed in their browser. The attacker gains control over the victim's session or steals sensitive information, depending on the exploit's objective.

Complex XSS exploits can also involve chaining multiple vulnerabilities together. For example, an attacker might first exploit an XSS vulnerability to inject a malicious script that steals a user's session cookie. They can then use this stolen session to impersonate the user and perform actions on their behalf within the application.

Another advanced technique is DOM-based XSS, where the payload manipulates the Document Object Model (DOM) of the web page to execute malicious code. This occurs entirely on the client-side and can be challenging to detect because the server-side code remains unaffected.

Security researchers and analysts deconstruct complex XSS exploits by analyzing the payload, identifying the obfuscation techniques used, and tracing the flow of execution within the victim's browser. This often involves using tools like web proxies, browser developer tools, and

JavaScript debugging tools to step through the code execution.

Additionally, sandboxing techniques can be employed to isolate and study the behavior of the malicious code without compromising the security of the analyst's environment. Sandboxing provides a controlled environment for executing the payload and observing its actions, allowing for a thorough analysis.

Understanding the intricacies of complex XSS exploits is essential for developing effective countermeasures. Security professionals can use this knowledge to improve input validation and output encoding in web applications, implement Content Security Policy (CSP) headers, and educate users about the risks of clicking on suspicious links.

Organizations should also stay informed about the latest trends and tactics used by attackers in the XSS landscape. Regularly updating security policies and conducting security training for development and operations teams is critical for maintaining a proactive defense against complex XSS attacks.

In summary, deconstructing complex XSS exploits is a fundamental aspect of web application security. These exploits showcase the creativity and persistence of attackers, making it crucial for defenders to keep pace with evolving techniques. By dissecting these exploits, security professionals can strengthen their understanding of XSS vulnerabilities and enhance their ability to protect web applications and their users.

Chapter 5: In-Depth Defense Against Direct Object References

Advanced approaches to detect and prevent Direct Object References (DOR) are essential for bolstering web application security. Direct Object References occur when a user can access and manipulate objects directly, such as files, databases, or other resources, by modifying input parameters or URLs. Attackers exploit DOR vulnerabilities to access unauthorized data or perform actions they should not be able to execute.

Detecting DOR vulnerabilities requires a comprehensive understanding of an application's data flow and access control mechanisms. Security professionals can use a combination of automated tools and manual testing to identify potential DOR issues. Automated scanners can help identify common DOR patterns, such as predictable URL structures or insufficient input validation. However, manual testing is often required to discover more complex and subtle vulnerabilities.

In advanced DOR detection, testers may use techniques like parameter tampering or changing URLs to see if they can access data or resources that should be restricted. They also analyze the application's source code to identify weak points in access control logic. For instance, if an application relies solely on client-side controls, attackers can manipulate these controls using tools like browser development tools or proxy servers.

Effective DOR prevention begins with robust access control mechanisms. Implementing proper authorization checks at the server-side is a fundamental step. Role-based access control (RBAC), attribute-based access control (ABAC), or other access control models can be employed to ensure that users can only access resources they are authorized to view or modify.

Another advanced approach to DOR prevention is the use of cryptographic techniques. Developers can employ techniques like tokenization or encryption to protect sensitive data and ensure that even if an attacker gains access to a reference, they cannot decipher its contents. Cryptographic protections can add an extra layer of security, especially when handling confidential or critical data.

Additionally, the use of unique identifiers for resources can mitigate DOR vulnerabilities. Instead of relying on predictable sequential IDs, which attackers can guess or manipulate, applications can use randomly generated, cryptographically secure identifiers. This makes it extremely challenging for attackers to guess valid references.

In advanced DOR prevention, implementing session management and session validation mechanisms is crucial. Ensuring that sessions are properly managed, and tokens are verified during each user interaction helps prevent unauthorized access to resources. Implementing robust session management practices can significantly reduce the risk of DOR vulnerabilities.

Web Application Firewalls (WAFs) can play a role in advanced DOR prevention. WAFs can be configured to detect and block suspicious URL patterns or parameter manipulations that may indicate DOR attacks. However, relying solely on WAFs is not a comprehensive solution, and they should complement other security measures.

Logging and monitoring are vital components of advanced DOR prevention. Regularly monitoring access logs and conducting security audits can help identify suspicious or unauthorized access attempts. Early detection of anomalous behavior can lead to prompt mitigation and prevent potential data breaches.

Education and awareness among development and operational teams are critical for advanced DOR prevention. Developers should be trained to implement secure coding practices, conduct code reviews, and understand the importance of proper access control. Operations teams should be aware of the risks associated with DOR vulnerabilities and monitor systems for any signs of exploitation.

Penetration testing and security assessments should be part of an organization's advanced DOR prevention strategy. Engaging ethical hackers or security experts to conduct thorough assessments can uncover hidden vulnerabilities and weaknesses in access control mechanisms.

In summary, advanced approaches to detect and prevent Direct Object References are essential for safeguarding web applications from unauthorized access and data breaches. These approaches include a combination of automated tools, manual testing, access control mechanisms, cryptographic techniques, session management, monitoring, education, and security assessments. By adopting a multi-layered approach to DOR prevention, organizations can significantly enhance their web application security posture and protect sensitive data from malicious actors.

Fine-tuning access control and authorization mechanisms is a critical aspect of web application security, as it determines who can access what resources within an application. Access control defines the rules and policies that govern what actions users, roles, or entities are allowed or denied. Authorization, on the other hand, is the process of verifying whether a user, role, or entity has the necessary permissions to perform a specific action or access a particular resource.

Effective access control and authorization mechanisms are essential for preventing unauthorized access, protecting sensitive data, and ensuring that users only have access to the resources and functionality that they are entitled to use. Fine-tuning these mechanisms involves several key considerations and best practices.

One of the fundamental principles of fine-tuning access control is the principle of least privilege. This principle dictates that users and roles should be granted the minimum level of access required to perform their tasks. By adhering to the principle of least privilege, organizations can reduce the attack surface and limit the potential impact of security breaches.

Role-based access control (RBAC) is a common approach to access control that involves defining roles within an application and assigning permissions to those roles. Fine-tuning RBAC involves carefully defining roles, mapping roles to specific permissions, and regularly reviewing and updating role assignments to ensure they align with the organization's security policies and evolving requirements.

Attribute-based access control (ABAC) is another approach that considers various attributes, such as user attributes, resource attributes, and environmental attributes, to make access control decisions. Fine-tuning ABAC involves defining and managing a set of policies that take into account these attributes and dynamically determine access rights based on specific conditions. To fine-tune access control and authorization mechanisms effectively, it's crucial to conduct a thorough analysis of the application's data flow and security requirements. This analysis helps identify the critical assets and resources that need protection and ensures that the access control policies are appropriately aligned with these assets. Role hierarchies can be a part of fine-tuning access control, especially in complex applications. Hierarchical roles can help streamline permissions management by allowing higher-level roles to inherit permissions from lower-level roles. Care must be taken when implementing role hierarchies to avoid unintended consequences or security loopholes.

Additionally, access control lists (ACLs) and access control matrices (ACMs) can be used to specify and fine-tune access control policies at a granular level. ACLs define which users or roles have access to specific resources, while ACMs provide a matrix-based approach to define access rights for various combinations of users and resources.

Fine-tuning access control mechanisms also involves considering authentication and session management. Strong authentication mechanisms, such as multi-factor authentication (MFA) or biometrics, can enhance the security of access control. Session management practices, like enforcing session timeouts and securely storing session tokens, contribute to preventing unauthorized access during active sessions.

Logging and monitoring play a crucial role in fine-tuning access control and authorization. Robust logging allows organizations to track and audit access events, providing insights into who accessed what resources and when. Real-time monitoring can detect suspicious or unauthorized access attempts, enabling rapid response and mitigation.

Regular access control reviews and assessments are essential for fine-tuning these mechanisms over time. Security teams should periodically review and update access control policies, roles, and permissions to align with changing business needs and evolving threats. Penetration testing and vulnerability assessments can help identify weaknesses in access control and authorization.

Finally, fine-tuning access control mechanisms should be an ongoing process, integrated into the software development lifecycle. Security should not be an afterthought but a fundamental consideration from the initial design phase through development, testing, deployment, and maintenance.

In summary, fine-tuning access control and authorization mechanisms is a critical aspect of web application security. Organizations should adhere to the principle of least privilege, leverage role-based and attribute-based access control, conduct thorough security analysis, implement role hierarchies, use ACLs and ACMs as needed, consider authentication and session management, implement logging and monitoring, conduct regular reviews and assessments, and integrate security into the development lifecycle. By following these best practices, organizations can enhance their access control and authorization mechanisms, reducing the risk of unauthorized access and data breaches.

Chapter 6: Advanced Security Configuration Techniques

Optimizing security configurations for maximum protection is a critical aspect of web application security, as improperly configured systems can introduce vulnerabilities and expose sensitive data to potential threats. Security configurations encompass a wide range of settings, from network and server configurations to application-specific security settings.

The process of optimizing security configurations involves fine-tuning these settings to align with security best practices and the specific requirements of an organization. Properly configured security settings can reduce the attack surface, minimize security risks, and enhance the overall security posture of a web application.

One of the first steps in optimizing security configurations is conducting a comprehensive risk assessment. This assessment helps identify potential security threats, vulnerabilities, and weaknesses in the existing configuration. By understanding the risks, organizations can prioritize and address the most critical security concerns.

In optimizing network and server configurations, organizations should follow the principle of least privilege, ensuring that only necessary services, ports, and protocols are enabled. Unnecessary services and ports should be disabled or closed to reduce the potential attack surface. Firewall rules should be configured to allow only legitimate traffic and block unauthorized access.

Encryption plays a significant role in security configurations. Organizations should enable encryption for data in transit using protocols like HTTPS and TLS. Additionally, data at rest should be encrypted to protect it from unauthorized access in case of data breaches or physical theft.

Secure authentication mechanisms are crucial in security configurations. Password policies should be enforced to ensure strong and unique passwords. Multi-factor authentication (MFA) should be implemented to add an extra layer of security. User account lockout policies can help prevent brute force attacks.

Web application security settings should also be optimized. This includes configuring security headers such as Content Security Policy (CSP), X-Content-Type-Options, and X-Frame-Options to mitigate common web vulnerabilities like cross-site scripting (XSS) and clickjacking. Security headers can instruct browsers on how to handle certain aspects of web content.

Intrusion detection and prevention systems (IDS/IPS) can be integrated into security configurations to monitor and block suspicious network activity. These systems can help detect and mitigate attacks in real-time, providing an additional layer of defense.

Patch management is a critical component of security configurations. Organizations should establish a process for regularly updating and patching operating systems, applications, and third-party software to address known vulnerabilities. Vulnerability scanning tools can assist in identifying missing patches.

Access control and authorization settings should align with the principle of least privilege. Users and roles should have the minimum level of access required to perform their tasks. Role-based access control (RBAC) and attribute-based access control (ABAC) can help define and enforce access policies.

Logging and auditing settings should be optimized to capture relevant security events and activities. Logs should be stored securely and regularly reviewed for signs of suspicious or unauthorized access. Security Information and Event Management (SIEM) systems can help centralize and analyze logs.

Regular security assessments and penetration testing should be conducted to identify weaknesses and vulnerabilities in security configurations. Ethical hackers can simulate real-world attacks to uncover potential risks that might not be apparent during routine testing.

Security configurations should also consider compliance requirements and industry standards. Organizations operating in regulated industries should ensure that their configurations align with the specific regulations and standards applicable to their business.

Finally, security configurations should be documented and maintained. Documentation helps ensure that security settings are consistent and can be audited for compliance. Regular reviews and updates are essential to adapt to evolving threats and vulnerabilities.

In summary, optimizing security configurations for maximum protection is a crucial aspect of web application security. This process involves fine-tuning network and server settings, enabling encryption, implementing secure authentication mechanisms, configuring web application security settings, integrating intrusion detection and prevention systems, managing patches, defining access control policies, optimizing logging and auditing, conducting security assessments, and considering compliance requirements. By following these best practices and maintaining a proactive security posture, organizations can enhance the security of their web applications and reduce the risk of security breaches and data compromises.

Securing your application is an ongoing process that requires a deep understanding of evolving threats and the implementation of advanced techniques to stay ahead of potential vulnerabilities. As attackers become more sophisticated, it's essential to employ strategies that go beyond basic security measures to protect your application and its sensitive data.

One advanced technique is threat modeling, which involves systematically identifying and evaluating potential threats and vulnerabilities in your application's design and architecture. Threat modeling allows you to prioritize security measures based on the most significant risks to your application, ensuring that your efforts are focused on the areas that need the most attention.

Secure coding practices are fundamental to application security. Advanced secure coding techniques involve using frameworks and libraries that are inherently secure, implementing security controls within your code, and following best practices such as input validation, output encoding, and using prepared statements to prevent SQL injection.

Consider implementing security by design principles, where security is integrated into every stage of the software development lifecycle. This approach involves considering security requirements from the initial design phase and throughout development, testing, deployment, and maintenance.

Security automation is a powerful advanced technique that can help you detect and respond to security threats more efficiently. Implement automated security testing, continuous integration, and continuous deployment pipelines to catch vulnerabilities early and streamline security processes.

Advanced threat detection and monitoring tools can provide real-time visibility into your application's security posture. These tools can detect abnormal behavior and security incidents, allowing you to respond quickly to potential threats and mitigate their impact.

Implementing strong access controls is crucial for advanced security. Fine-grained access control mechanisms, such as role-based access control (RBAC) and attribute-based access control (ABAC), can help ensure that users have the minimum level of access required to perform their tasks.

User authentication and authorization should be reinforced with advanced techniques such as multi-factor authentication (MFA), single sign-on (SSO), and token-based authentication. These methods add additional layers of security to protect user accounts and sensitive data.

Secure session management is essential for preventing session-related attacks, such as session fixation and session hijacking. Advanced techniques include using secure session tokens, enforcing session timeouts, and implementing secure logout processes.

Advanced encryption techniques should be used to protect data at rest and in transit. Implement strong encryption algorithms and key management practices to safeguard sensitive information from unauthorized access. Security information and event management (SIEM) systems can provide advanced capabilities for analyzing and correlating security events. These systems can help you detect and respond to security incidents more effectively by aggregating and analyzing log data from various sources.

Consider implementing a web application firewall (WAF) as an advanced security layer to protect against common web application attacks, including SQL injection, cross-site scripting (XSS), and cross-site request forgery (CSRF).

Regular security assessments and penetration testing should be performed to identify vulnerabilities that may not be apparent during routine testing. Advanced security testing techniques, such as fuzz testing and threat emulation, can simulate sophisticated attacks to uncover potential weaknesses.

Implementing a robust incident response plan is essential for advanced security. This plan should outline the steps to take in the event of a security incident, including containment, eradication, and recovery procedures.

Security awareness training for your development and operations teams is a crucial advanced technique. Educating your staff about security best practices and the latest threats can help them recognize and respond to potential risks effectively.

Consider integrating security into your DevOps practices by implementing DevSecOps. This approach emphasizes security as an integral part of the development and deployment pipeline, ensuring that security is not an afterthought but an ongoing concern.

Secure code reviews and peer reviews can help identify security issues in your application code. Encourage team members to review each other's code for security vulnerabilities and share knowledge about secure coding practices.

Implementing advanced security monitoring and incident response automation can help reduce response times and improve overall security posture. Consider using machine learning and artificial intelligence techniques to analyze security events and detect anomalies.

Regularly update and patch all components of your application, including third-party libraries and dependencies. Vulnerability management should be an ongoing process to address newly discovered security issues.

In summary, securing your application requires advanced techniques that go beyond basic security measures. Threat modeling, secure coding practices, security by design, automation, access controls, advanced authentication, secure session management, encryption, SIEM, WAF, security assessments, incident response planning, training, DevSecOps, code reviews, and vulnerability management are all essential components of advanced application security. By implementing these techniques and staying vigilant against evolving threats, you can protect your application and its users from potential security risks.

Chapter 7: Cutting-Edge Strategies for Cross-Site Request Forgery (CSRF) Protection

In recent years, CSRF protection has seen significant advancements, driven by the ever-evolving landscape of web application security threats. These developments aim to provide more robust and comprehensive defense mechanisms against cross-site request forgery attacks, which continue to pose a serious risk to web applications and their users.

One notable advancement is the adoption of state-of-the-art anti-CSRF tokens. Traditional CSRF tokens have been effective in mitigating basic CSRF attacks by generating a random token for each user session and including it in forms or AJAX requests. However, attackers have found ways to bypass these protections.

To address this issue, modern web applications now utilize advanced anti-CSRF tokens that incorporate additional factors such as the user's session ID, the request's origin, and cryptographic techniques. These tokens are more challenging for attackers to forge, making it significantly more difficult to execute successful CSRF attacks.

Additionally, some frameworks and libraries have introduced built-in CSRF protection mechanisms that automatically generate and validate anti-CSRF tokens. This simplifies the implementation of CSRF defenses for developers, reducing the risk of misconfiguration or oversight.

Another key advancement in CSRF protection is the adoption of the SameSite attribute for cookies. The SameSite attribute allows developers to specify whether a cookie should be sent with cross-origin requests. By setting the SameSite attribute to "Strict" or "Lax," developers can mitigate CSRF attacks that rely on cookie-based authentication.

The "Strict" option prevents cookies from being sent in cross-origin requests, ensuring that they are only sent when the request originates from the same site. On the other hand, the "Lax" option allows cookies to be sent in top-level navigations initiated by a link click, ensuring a balance between security and user experience.

Modern web browsers have also played a crucial role in CSRF protection advancements. They have started to enforce stricter security policies by default, which include SameSite attribute enforcement and stricter CORS (Cross-Origin Resource Sharing) rules. These browser-level protections make it more challenging for attackers to exploit CSRF vulnerabilities.

Furthermore, the use of Content Security Policy (CSP) headers has gained popularity as an advanced CSRF mitigation technique. CSP allows developers to define a set of trusted sources from which resources (such as scripts, stylesheets, and images) can be loaded. By limiting the sources from which scripts can be executed, CSP can prevent the execution of malicious scripts injected via CSRF attacks.

Web application security standards and guidelines, such as those provided by the Open Web Application Security Project (OWASP), have continuously evolved to include the latest CSRF protection best practices. Developers and security professionals can refer to these resources to stay up-to-date with the latest advancements and recommended techniques.

Furthermore, modern web application frameworks and libraries often include built-in CSRF protection features that developers can leverage. These frameworks provide developers with tools and functions to automatically generate, validate, and manage anti-CSRF tokens, reducing the complexity of implementing CSRF defenses.

In addition to these advancements in prevention, the detection and reporting of CSRF vulnerabilities have also improved. Security researchers and organizations are continuously conducting security assessments and penetration testing to identify and report CSRF vulnerabilities in web applications. These findings help developers and organizations proactively address CSRF issues before they can be exploited by malicious actors.

Security automation tools have become more sophisticated in identifying and mitigating CSRF vulnerabilities. These tools can simulate CSRF attacks, evaluate the effectiveness of anti-CSRF defenses, and provide actionable recommendations for improving protection.

Furthermore, organizations are increasingly adopting bug bounty programs and responsible disclosure practices, encouraging security researchers to report CSRF vulnerabilities in exchange for rewards or recognition. This collaborative approach helps identify and resolve CSRF issues before they can be exploited by cybercriminals.

In summary, CSRF protection has witnessed significant advancements in recent years, driven by the evolving threat landscape and the dedication of security professionals and researchers. These advancements include the adoption of advanced anti-CSRF tokens, the use of the SameSite attribute for cookies, browser-level security enhancements, Content Security Policy (CSP), security standards and guidelines, built-in CSRF protection in web frameworks, improved detection and reporting, and the use of security automation tools. These developments collectively contribute to a more secure web environment, reducing the risk of CSRF attacks and enhancing the protection of web applications and their users.

In the ever-evolving landscape of web security, advanced strategies are essential to counter the growing sophistication of Cross-Site Request Forgery (CSRF) attacks. These strategies focus on not only mitigating existing CSRF vulnerabilities but also anticipating and defending against emerging attack vectors that malicious actors may exploit.

One key approach to countering evolving CSRF attacks is the implementation of user-specific anti-CSRF tokens. Traditional CSRF tokens are generated per-session and remain constant throughout a user's session. However, attackers have exploited this predictability by devising methods to steal or forge these tokens. To address this, modern applications generate unique tokens for each user, often combining session data, user-specific information, and cryptographic techniques. By doing so, even if an attacker manages to steal one user's token, it cannot be used to forge requests on behalf of another user.

Furthermore, some organizations have adopted the practice of refreshing anti-CSRF tokens with every request. This approach, known as per-request tokens, ensures that each request sent by the user includes a fresh token. In this way, the token's lifespan is reduced to a single request, making it virtually impossible for an attacker to obtain and reuse it.

Implementing dynamic anti-CSRF tokens is another advanced strategy. Instead of generating tokens at the beginning of a user's session, dynamic tokens are created on-the-fly for each form submission or request. These tokens are typically short-lived and tied to the specific action being performed. This ensures that tokens remain unpredictable and secure, as they cannot be reused for other actions.

In addition to advanced token generation techniques, developers should consider incorporating secure, randomized identifiers into the application's URLs. This can help protect against CSRF attacks that target URL parameters or rely on predictable URLs for exploitation. These random identifiers can be challenging for attackers to predict or manipulate, enhancing overall security.

Another advanced defense against CSRF attacks involves the use of custom headers. Developers can employ custom HTTP headers, such as the X-Requested-With header, to differentiate between legitimate and malicious requests. By checking for the presence of these headers in server-side code, developers can reject requests that lack the required headers, effectively blocking CSRF attacks.

Furthermore, advanced web frameworks and libraries offer built-in CSRF protection mechanisms that automatically generate, validate, and manage anti-CSRF tokens. These frameworks simplify the implementation of CSRF defenses, reducing the risk of developer error or oversight. Leveraging these built-in features can save time and resources while bolstering security.

Browser security enhancements have also contributed to the defense against evolving CSRF attacks. For instance, the introduction of the SameSite attribute for cookies has become a valuable tool. Developers can use this attribute to specify whether a cookie should be sent with cross-origin requests, reducing the risk of CSRF attacks that target cookie-based authentication.

Modern browsers are becoming increasingly vigilant when it comes to enforcing security policies related to cross-origin requests and cookies. Developers should stay informed about these evolving browser security features and adopt best practices to align with them.

Furthermore, the adoption of Content Security Policy (CSP) headers can provide additional layers of protection. CSP allows developers to define which sources are trusted for loading resources, such as scripts and stylesheets. By limiting the sources from which scripts can be executed, CSP can prevent the execution of malicious scripts injected via CSRF attacks.

Continuous security testing is paramount in countering evolving CSRF attacks. Organizations should regularly perform vulnerability assessments, penetration testing, and security code reviews to identify and rectify potential weaknesses in their applications. Automated security scanning tools can assist in detecting and mitigating CSRF vulnerabilities.

Bug bounty programs and responsible disclosure practices remain crucial in the ongoing defense against CSRF attacks. Encouraging security researchers to report vulnerabilities and rewarding them for their findings can help organizations uncover and address CSRF issues before they are exploited maliciously.

In summary, advanced strategies are indispensable in countering the evolving threat landscape of CSRF attacks. These strategies encompass user-specific anti-CSRF tokens, per-request tokens, dynamic token generation, randomized identifiers in URLs, custom headers, built-in CSRF protection in web frameworks, browser security enhancements like the SameSite attribute, Content Security Policy (CSP) headers, continuous security testing, and collaborative security initiatives such as bug bounty programs. By adopting and adapting these measures, organizations can stay ahead of CSRF attackers and fortify their web applications against evolving threats.

Chapter 8: Proactive Component Management and Vulnerability Mitigation

Proactively managing vulnerable components is a critical aspect of web application security, as it helps organizations stay ahead of potential threats and reduce the risk of security breaches. Vulnerable components can include libraries, frameworks, third-party plugins, or any code that an application relies on. By taking a proactive approach, organizations can strengthen their security posture and enhance the resilience of their applications.

One of the first steps in proactively managing vulnerable components is to establish a comprehensive inventory of all components used within an application. This includes not only the primary programming languages and frameworks but also any third-party dependencies and libraries. Maintaining a detailed record of components is essential for tracking vulnerabilities and ensuring that updates are applied promptly.

Once an inventory is in place, organizations can leverage various tools and resources to continuously monitor for vulnerabilities in their components. Vulnerability databases and security feeds, such as the National Vulnerability Database (NVD) and the Common Vulnerabilities and Exposures (CVE) system, provide up-to-date information about known security issues. Automated vulnerability scanners and software composition analysis tools can also help identify vulnerabilities in components used by the application.

Regularly reviewing and analyzing the information from these sources allows organizations to assess the severity and impact of vulnerabilities in their components. This assessment is crucial for prioritizing which vulnerabilities to address first, as not all vulnerabilities pose the same level of risk. Vulnerabilities that have a high severity rating and are actively exploited by attackers should be addressed as a top priority.

Once vulnerabilities are identified and prioritized, organizations should establish a clear and efficient process for remediation. This process should include steps for verifying the vulnerability, assessing its impact on the application, and determining the appropriate mitigation strategy. In some cases, mitigation may involve applying patches or updates provided by the component's maintainers. In other cases, organizations may need to implement workarounds or temporarily disable vulnerable components while seeking alternative solutions.

It's essential to keep the component inventory and vulnerability management process up to date. As new components are introduced or existing ones are updated, they should be added to the inventory, and their vulnerabilities should be assessed. Additionally, organizations should regularly review their mitigation strategies to ensure they remain effective in the face of evolving threats.

In some instances, organizations may find that certain components are no longer actively maintained or have a history of frequent vulnerabilities. In such cases, it may be necessary to consider alternative components or develop in-house solutions to reduce reliance on the vulnerable component. This proactive approach reduces the long-term risk associated with maintaining insecure dependencies.

A critical aspect of proactively managing vulnerable components is establishing clear communication and collaboration between development and security teams. Security professionals should work closely with developers to provide guidance on identifying and addressing vulnerabilities. Development teams should be encouraged to report any vulnerabilities or potential security issues they encounter during the development process.

Additionally, organizations should implement a robust change management process that includes thorough testing and validation of updates and patches before they are deployed to production environments. This ensures that the remediation efforts do not introduce new issues or disrupt the application's functionality.

Furthermore, it's essential to stay informed about the latest developments in the security landscape. By actively monitoring security news, attending conferences, and participating in industry forums, organizations can gain insights into emerging threats and best practices for vulnerability management.

Proactively managing vulnerable components is an ongoing process that requires dedication and vigilance. It is not a one-time task but rather a fundamental aspect of maintaining a secure web application. By establishing a comprehensive component inventory, continuously monitoring for vulnerabilities, prioritizing remediation efforts, fostering collaboration between teams, and staying informed about emerging threats, organizations can reduce their exposure to security risks and strengthen their overall security posture.

In summary, proactively managing vulnerable components is a critical practice for enhancing web application security. This proactive approach involves establishing a comprehensive component inventory, continuously monitoring for vulnerabilities, prioritizing remediation efforts, fostering collaboration between development and security teams, and staying informed about emerging threats. By implementing these strategies and maintaining a proactive mindset, organizations can reduce the risk of security breaches and better protect their web applications.

Comprehensive vulnerability mitigation techniques are essential components of an effective web application security strategy. These techniques are designed to address a wide range of security vulnerabilities that can potentially be exploited by attackers. By implementing a comprehensive approach to vulnerability mitigation, organizations can significantly reduce the risk of security breaches and protect their web applications and sensitive data.

One fundamental aspect of comprehensive vulnerability mitigation is conducting regular security assessments and audits of web applications. This involves using various testing methodologies, such as vulnerability scanning, penetration testing, and code reviews, to identify potential vulnerabilities in the application's code, configuration, and architecture. These assessments should be conducted both during the development process and periodically after the application is in production.

Identifying vulnerabilities is just the first step; the next crucial phase is to prioritize and remediate them effectively. Not all vulnerabilities pose the same level of risk, and organizations must allocate resources based on the severity and potential impact of each vulnerability. Vulnerabilities with a high severity rating and a higher likelihood of exploitation should be addressed as a top priority.

One effective mitigation technique is the principle of least privilege, which involves restricting user and system permissions to the minimum necessary for performing specific tasks. By implementing the principle of least privilege, organizations can limit the potential damage that can be caused by attackers who exploit vulnerabilities. This technique applies not only to user access but also to application components and services.

Another essential aspect of comprehensive vulnerability mitigation is keeping software and systems up to date. This includes applying security patches and updates provided by software vendors and maintaining a current version of all components and libraries used by the application. Many vulnerabilities can be mitigated simply by ensuring that systems are running the latest secure versions of software.

Secure coding practices play a significant role in vulnerability mitigation. Developers should be trained in secure coding principles and follow best practices when writing code. This includes input validation, output encoding, and avoiding common coding mistakes that can lead to vulnerabilities, such as SQL injection or cross-site scripting (XSS).

Security headers and mechanisms, such as Content Security Policy (CSP), can be effective in mitigating specific types of vulnerabilities, particularly those related to XSS attacks. CSP allows organizations to define a policy that specifies which sources of content are considered trusted and can be executed by the browser. This helps prevent malicious scripts from executing in the context of the web application.

Web application firewalls (WAFs) are another valuable tool for comprehensive vulnerability mitigation. WAFs can intercept and filter incoming traffic to the web application, blocking known attack patterns and providing an additional layer of defense. However, it's essential to configure WAFs correctly to avoid false positives and ensure they effectively protect against known threats.

Security monitoring and incident response are integral components of comprehensive vulnerability mitigation. Organizations should implement robust monitoring solutions that can detect suspicious activities and potential security breaches. When a security incident occurs, having a well-defined incident response plan in place allows organizations to respond swiftly and effectively to minimize the impact and mitigate vulnerabilities that may have been exploited.

Regular security awareness training for employees is essential to ensure that everyone in the organization understands the importance of security and is aware of potential vulnerabilities and attack vectors. Employees should be trained to recognize and report security incidents promptly.

Encryption and secure communication practices are vital for protecting sensitive data and mitigating vulnerabilities related to data breaches. Implementing encryption for data in transit and data at rest, using strong encryption algorithms and secure protocols, helps ensure that data remains confidential and secure.

Comprehensive vulnerability mitigation techniques also involve threat modeling and risk assessment. Organizations should identify potential threats and vulnerabilities specific to their web applications and assess the potential impact and likelihood of exploitation. This information can guide mitigation efforts and resource allocation.

Lastly, organizations should stay informed about the latest security threats and vulnerabilities relevant to their web applications. Subscribing to security mailing lists, following industry news, and participating in security communities can provide valuable insights into emerging threats and mitigation techniques.

In summary, comprehensive vulnerability mitigation techniques are essential for ensuring the security of web applications. These techniques encompass a range of practices, including regular security assessments, prioritization of vulnerabilities, secure coding practices, least privilege principles, software and system updates, security headers and mechanisms, web application firewalls, monitoring and incident response, security awareness training, encryption, threat modeling, and staying informed about emerging threats. By implementing these techniques, organizations can significantly reduce the risk of security breaches and protect their web applications and data.

Chapter 9: Real-World Case Studies and Lessons Learned

Real-life web application security incidents serve as powerful lessons for organizations, illustrating the critical importance of robust security measures. These incidents, often involving high-profile breaches and their aftermath, shed light on the vulnerabilities that can be exploited by malicious actors and emphasize the need for proactive security practices.

One such incident was the Equifax data breach in 2017, where attackers exploited a known vulnerability in the Apache Struts web application framework to gain access to sensitive customer data. This breach exposed the personal information of nearly 147 million people and underscored the significant risks associated with unpatched vulnerabilities.

Another notable incident involved the breach of the Office of Personnel Management (OPM) in 2015, where attackers compromised sensitive background investigation records of millions of current and former government employees. This incident highlighted the vulnerabilities within government systems and raised questions about the security of sensitive government data.

The Yahoo data breaches in 2013 and 2014 were among the largest data breaches in history, affecting billions of user accounts. Attackers exploited web application vulnerabilities to gain unauthorized access to Yahoo's user database, demonstrating the far-reaching consequences of inadequate security measures.

In 2018, the Facebook-Cambridge Analytica scandal made headlines worldwide. While not a traditional data breach, it revealed how third-party applications could access and misuse user data on a massive scale. This incident highlighted the importance of user data privacy and the need for strict access controls.

The Ticketmaster data breach in 2018 was another significant incident where attackers injected malicious code into the company's web application, compromising customer payment information. This incident showcased the risks associated with supply chain attacks and the need for comprehensive security monitoring.

Ransomware attacks on healthcare organizations, such as the WannaCry and NotPetya incidents in 2017, disrupted critical healthcare services and compromised patient records. These incidents emphasized the importance of securing web applications used in the healthcare sector to protect patient data and ensure uninterrupted care.

The Capital One data breach in 2019 exposed the personal information of millions of customers and highlighted the risks associated with cloud-based storage and misconfigured web application firewalls. This incident served as a wake-up call for organizations to secure their cloud infrastructure effectively.

In 2020, the SolarWinds supply chain attack impacted numerous organizations, including government agencies and major corporations. While not a web application breach per se, it demonstrated the ripple effects of a single vulnerability in a trusted software vendor's product and the need for rigorous security assessments of third-party software.

The Colonial Pipeline ransomware attack in 2021 disrupted fuel supply across the Eastern United States, underscoring the critical infrastructure's vulnerability to cyberattacks. While the attack targeted operational technology systems, it highlighted the interconnectedness of web applications and critical infrastructure.

The Log4j vulnerability (CVE-2021-44228) in the Apache Log4j library in late 2021 sent shockwaves through the cybersecurity community. It allowed attackers to execute arbitrary code remotely, potentially compromising web applications and servers globally. Organizations scrambled to patch affected systems to prevent exploitation.

These real-life web application security incidents illustrate that no organization is immune to cyber threats. They emphasize the need for continuous monitoring, timely patching of vulnerabilities, robust access controls, and incident response plans. Moreover, they serve as a stark reminder that the consequences of security breaches can be severe, including financial losses, damage to reputation, and legal consequences.

In summary, real-life web application security incidents have left a lasting impact on the cybersecurity landscape. They have revealed vulnerabilities and weaknesses that organizations must address to protect their systems and data effectively. These incidents serve as valuable case studies for understanding the evolving threat landscape and the importance of proactive security measures.

Security incidents, whether involving web applications or other aspects of cybersecurity, offer valuable lessons and key takeaways for organizations striving to enhance their security posture. These incidents, often costly and disruptive, underscore the importance of proactive measures and continuous vigilance in the face of evolving threats.

One of the fundamental lessons from security incidents is that no organization is immune to cyber threats. Whether you're a small business or a multinational corporation, the potential for breaches and vulnerabilities exists. As such, organizations of all sizes must prioritize security as an ongoing process rather than a one-time task.

The Equifax breach in 2017 serves as a stark example of the consequences of failing to patch known vulnerabilities promptly. In this case, attackers exploited a vulnerability in an outdated software component, leading to a massive data breach. The lesson here is clear: timely patching and vulnerability management are critical to preventing security incidents.

Effective incident response is another key takeaway from security incidents. Organizations must have a well-defined incident response plan in place, specifying roles, responsibilities, and procedures for responding to security breaches. A rapid response can mitigate the damage and limit the exposure of sensitive data.

The Yahoo data breaches in 2013 and 2014 demonstrated the importance of thorough forensic investigations. Understanding the scope and nature of a breach is crucial for implementing effective remediation measures and preventing future incidents. Forensic analysis helps organizations identify the root causes and patterns of attacks.

Access control and authentication practices are central to security, as highlighted by incidents like the Office of Personnel Management (OPM) breach in 2015. Strong authentication, access controls, and the principle of least privilege should be integral parts of an organization's security strategy.

The Facebook-Cambridge Analytica scandal underscored the significance of data privacy and responsible data handling. Organizations must be transparent about how they collect, use, and share user data, complying with applicable data protection regulations. Building user trust is essential for long-term success.

Supply chain security became a focal point after the Ticketmaster breach in 2018. Organizations must evaluate the security practices of their third-party vendors and suppliers, as vulnerabilities in their systems can affect the entire supply chain. Conducting security assessments and due diligence is crucial when integrating third-party services or software.

The Colonial Pipeline ransomware attack in 2021 revealed the vulnerabilities in critical infrastructure. Organizations operating critical systems should prioritize cybersecurity measures and regularly assess their readiness to withstand cyber threats. Cyberattacks on critical infrastructure can have far-reaching consequences.

The SolarWinds supply chain attack demonstrated the potential for cascading effects when a trusted vendor's software is compromised. Organizations need to evaluate and secure their software supply chains, considering the integrity of third-party software components.

The Log4j vulnerability in 2021 highlighted the importance of proactive vulnerability management. Organizations should be proactive in identifying and patching vulnerabilities in their software stack, especially in widely used libraries and components.

Security incidents also underscore the need for comprehensive security awareness training for employees. Human error remains a significant contributor to security breaches, and educating personnel about cybersecurity best practices is essential.

Lastly, lessons from security incidents reinforce the importance of continuous monitoring and threat intelligence. Security teams should stay informed about emerging threats and vulnerabilities to adapt their defenses effectively.

In summary, security incidents offer valuable lessons for organizations aiming to strengthen their security posture. Key takeaways include the need for proactive measures, timely patching, effective incident response, access control, data privacy, supply chain security, critical infrastructure protection, software supply chain integrity, vulnerability management, employee training, and continuous monitoring. By applying these lessons, organizations can better protect their assets, data, and reputation in an increasingly complex threat landscape.

Chapter 10: Future Trends in Web Application Security and Best Practices

Predicting the future of web application security is an endeavor that requires a deep understanding of evolving technology trends, threat landscapes, and user behaviors. As technology continues to advance at an unprecedented pace, so do the methods and tactics employed by cybercriminals seeking to exploit vulnerabilities in web applications.

One of the key trends in web application security is the increasing sophistication of cyberattacks. Attackers are continuously refining their techniques, making it essential for organizations to adopt more robust security measures. Advanced Persistent Threats (APTs) are becoming more prevalent, posing long-term threats to web applications and their users.

Machine learning and artificial intelligence (AI) are poised to play a significant role in the future of web application security. These technologies can help in the early detection of anomalies and suspicious activities, enabling quicker responses to potential threats. However, they can also be used by attackers to develop more advanced attack vectors, leading to a constant cat-and-mouse game between defenders and adversaries.

The proliferation of Internet of Things (IoT) devices presents a new set of challenges for web application security. As these devices become increasingly interconnected and integrated into web applications, they create additional attack surfaces that must be protected.

IoT security will require a combination of device-level security and robust application security practices.

The adoption of cloud computing and serverless architectures is reshaping how web applications are built and deployed. While these technologies offer scalability and flexibility, they also introduce new security considerations. Organizations must ensure that their cloud-based web applications are configured and secured correctly to prevent data breaches and unauthorized access. Web application programming languages and frameworks are continuously evolving. As new languages and frameworks gain popularity, they bring both advantages and vulnerabilities. Developers and security professionals must stay up-to-date with the latest developments and best practices to secure web applications effectively. The integration of DevOps and DevSecOps practices into the software development lifecycle is becoming the norm. This approach emphasizes the importance of security from the early stages of development, with security teams collaborating closely with developers to identify and address vulnerabilities before they reach production environments.

The adoption of Zero Trust security models is gaining traction in the web application security landscape. Zero Trust assumes that threats may already exist inside or outside the network, and access is only granted based on strict identity verification and continuous monitoring. This approach can significantly enhance web application security.

Privacy regulations, such as the General Data Protection Regulation (GDPR) and the California Consumer Privacy Act (CCPA), continue to evolve and expand globally.

Organizations must comply with these regulations by implementing robust data protection measures and ensuring user consent and data handling practices are in line with legal requirements.

Web application security testing and assessment methodologies are evolving to keep pace with emerging threats. Organizations are increasingly adopting automated security testing tools, such as dynamic and static application security testing (DAST and SAST), as well as interactive application security testing (IAST) and container security scanning.

Threat intelligence sharing and collaboration among organizations and security communities are becoming more critical. Sharing information about emerging threats and vulnerabilities helps organizations prepare and defend against potential attacks. Open-source threat intelligence platforms are gaining popularity as a means of facilitating information sharing.

The convergence of web application security and API security is becoming increasingly important. As web applications rely on APIs for data exchange and functionality, securing APIs is essential to overall application security. API security practices, such as authentication, authorization, and rate limiting, will be central to protecting web applications.

Quantum computing poses a potential future threat to web application security. While quantum computing offers incredible computational power, it could potentially break current encryption algorithms. Organizations need to prepare for the advent of quantum-resistant encryption methods to protect sensitive data.

The rise of decentralized technologies, such as blockchain and decentralized applications (dApps), introduces a new set of security challenges. While blockchain offers inherent security benefits, dApps must be designed and implemented with security in mind to prevent vulnerabilities and smart contract exploits.

As more web applications collect and process user data, the risk of data breaches and privacy violations continues to grow. The future of web application security will involve a focus on data protection, encryption, and secure data handling practices to safeguard user information.

In summary, predicting the future of web application security is a complex task that requires vigilance, adaptability, and a forward-thinking approach. Organizations must continuously evolve their security strategies, leverage emerging technologies, and stay informed about the latest threats and trends to protect their web applications and user data effectively. The future of web application security will be shaped by advancements in cyber threats, technology, and regulatory requirements, making it a dynamic and ever-evolving field. Preparing for emerging threats is a critical aspect of maintaining robust web application security. As the threat landscape evolves and cybercriminals develop new tactics, organizations must adapt and implement best practices to stay ahead of potential vulnerabilities and attacks. A fundamental best practice for preparing against emerging threats is to maintain a proactive and vigilant security posture. This involves regularly assessing your web applications and their components to identify vulnerabilities and weaknesses. Conducting thorough security assessments, such as penetration testing and vulnerability scanning, helps in uncovering potential issues before they can be exploited. Furthermore, organizations should keep a close eye on security advisories and alerts from trusted sources, including security organizations, government agencies, and software vendors. These alerts provide valuable information about newly discovered vulnerabilities and emerging threats.

To effectively prepare for emerging threats, organizations should establish a well-defined incident response plan. This plan outlines the steps to take in case of a security breach or an emerging threat. It should include clear roles and responsibilities for incident response team members, communication protocols, and escalation procedures. Regularly testing and updating this plan ensures that the organization can respond promptly and efficiently to any security incident.

Another best practice is to maintain a thorough inventory of all components and dependencies used in your web applications. This includes libraries, frameworks, and third-party services. Knowing what components are in use allows organizations to quickly assess and respond to vulnerabilities when they are discovered.

Security awareness and training for employees and developers are essential components of preparing for emerging threats. Educating staff about the latest security risks and best practices helps create a security-conscious culture within the organization. Developers should receive training on secure coding practices to minimize the introduction of vulnerabilities during the development process.

Implementing a robust access control and authentication mechanism is crucial for web application security. By ensuring that only authorized users can access sensitive resources and data, organizations can mitigate the risk of unauthorized access and data breaches. Emerging threats often target weak authentication and authorization systems, so strengthening these components is paramount.

Regularly applying security patches and updates to your web application stack is a fundamental practice for staying protected against known vulnerabilities. Attackers frequently target systems with outdated software and unpatched vulnerabilities, making patch management a critical part of security preparation.

Incorporating threat modeling into the development process can help identify potential security weaknesses early in the design phase. Threat modeling involves analyzing the application's architecture and identifying possible threats and vulnerabilities. By addressing these issues during development, organizations can reduce the risk of emerging threats later in the application's lifecycle.

Organizations should consider implementing a web application firewall (WAF) as part of their security strategy. A WAF can provide an additional layer of defense against emerging threats by monitoring and filtering incoming traffic for malicious activity. It can help mitigate various types of attacks, including SQL injection, cross-site scripting (XSS), and more.

Secure coding practices should be at the forefront of web application development. Developers should follow established coding standards and guidelines that emphasize security. This includes input validation, output encoding, and secure storage of sensitive data. Code reviews and static analysis tools can assist in identifying and addressing security issues during development.

Security testing should be an ongoing practice, not just a one-time event. Regularly conducting security assessments, such as penetration testing and code reviews, helps organizations identify and remediate vulnerabilities that may have been introduced or overlooked during development.

Additionally, organizations should consider implementing continuous monitoring and threat detection solutions. These tools can provide real-time visibility into the security posture of web applications and help identify suspicious activities or emerging threats promptly. Advanced analytics and machine learning can aid in detecting patterns indicative of security incidents.

Collaboration within the cybersecurity community is essential when preparing for emerging threats. Sharing threat intelligence and best practices with peers and industry groups can provide valuable insights into the latest threats and mitigation strategies. Many organizations participate in Information Sharing and Analysis Centers (ISACs) or similar information-sharing initiatives.

Lastly, staying informed about emerging threats through industry news, research reports, and conferences is essential for proactive security preparation. Cybersecurity is an ever-evolving field, and organizations must continuously adapt to new challenges and risks. By staying educated and implementing best practices, organizations can better protect their web applications from emerging threats and maintain a strong security posture.

Conclusion

In this comprehensive book bundle, "OWASP Top 10 Vulnerabilities," we embarked on a journey to explore the critical realm of web application security. Our collection of four distinct books covers a wide spectrum of knowledge, catering to beginners and experts alike.

In "Book 1 - Web Application Security 101: A Beginner's Guide to OWASP Top 10 Vulnerabilities," we laid the foundation for understanding the fundamental security risks faced by web applications. We provided essential insights into the OWASP Top 10 vulnerabilities, ensuring that readers with little to no prior experience could grasp the basics of web application security.

"Book 2 - Mastering OWASP Top 10: A Comprehensive Guide to Web Application Security" took our readers on a deeper dive into the world of web application security. We provided a comprehensive guide for those seeking to enhance their understanding and expertise in tackling the OWASP Top 10 vulnerabilities. This book served as a valuable resource for both intermediate and advanced security practitioners.

"Book 3 - Advanced Web Application Security: Beyond the OWASP Top 10" ventured into uncharted territories beyond the well-known OWASP Top 10 list. We explored advanced security concepts, emerging threats, and in-depth mitigation strategies, making it an indispensable resource for security professionals seeking to fortify their web applications.

In our final installment, "Book 4 - The Ultimate OWASP Top 10 Handbook: Expert Insights and Mitigation Strategies," we delved into the minds of industry experts. Their invaluable insights and real-world experiences provided readers with a unique perspective on handling web application security challenges. This book served as a bridge between theoretical knowledge and practical application, enabling readers to implement effective mitigation strategies.

Throughout this book bundle, we highlighted the significance of web application security, from its basics to its most advanced aspects. We stressed the importance of staying ahead of emerging threats, continuously adapting to the evolving threat landscape, and fostering a security-conscious culture within organizations.

As we conclude this journey through the "OWASP Top 10 Vulnerabilities" book bundle, we hope that readers of all backgrounds have gained a deeper understanding of web application security. Whether you are just beginning your journey into the world of cybersecurity or are a seasoned professional, we believe that the knowledge shared within these pages will empower you to protect web applications effectively.

Remember that web application security is not a destination but a continuous journey. The insights and strategies presented in these books will serve as a solid foundation for your ongoing efforts to safeguard the digital world. Stay vigilant, stay informed, and continue to evolve with the ever-changing landscape of web application security. Together, we can make the digital realm safer for all.